Becoming a Child of the Buddhas

Becoming a Child
of the Buddhas

*A Simple Clarification of the Root Verses
of Seven Point Mind Training*

Gomo Tulku

◆

THE VERY INSTANT THAT A MISERABLE BEING BOUND
IN THE PRISON OF CYCLIC EXISTENCE GENERATES THE
MIND OF ENLIGHTENMENT, HE BECOMES A CHILD OF
THOSE GONE TO BLISS AND AN OBJECT OF THE VEN-
ERATION OF WORLDLY GODS AND HUMAN BEINGS.

Shantideva

Translation of Gomo Tulku's text *Annotations to the Root Verses
of Mind Training* (bLo sbyong rtsa tshig la mchan 'grel)
and editing of the oral commentary by Joan Nicell.

Wisdom Publications • Boston

WISDOM PUBLICATIONS
199 ELM STREET
SOMERVILLE, MASSACHUSETTS 02144
USA

Library of Congress Cataloging-in-Publication Data

Gomo Tulku, 1922-1985.
    Becoming a child of the buddhas : a simple clarification
of the Root verses of seven point mind training / Gomo Tulku ;
translation of Gomo Tulku's text Annotations to the Root verses
of mind training (Blo sbyong rtsa tshig la mchan 'grel) and editing
of the oral commentary by Joan Nicell.
        p.   cm.
    Includes bibliographical references and index.
    ISBN 0-86171-139-4 (alk. paper)
    1. Ye-śes-rdo-rje, 'Chad-kha-ba. Theg pa chen po 'i gdams ṅag blo
sbyoṅ don bdun ma 'i rtsa ba. 2. Blo-Bzaṅ-'jam-dbyaṅs-smon-lam, Ke'u
-tshaṅ Sprul-sku, 18th cent. Blo sbyoṅ rtsa tshig. 3. Spiritual
life—Bka '-gdams-pa (Sect) 4. Dge-lugs-pa (Sect)—Doctrines.
I. Nicell, Joan. II. Ye-śes-rdo-rje, 'Chad-kha-ba. Theg pa chen
po 'i gdams ṅag blo sbyoṅ don bdun ma 'i rtsa ba. III. Blo-bzaṅ-'jam
-dbyaṅs-smon-lam, Ke 'u-tshaṅ Sprul-sku, 18th cent. Blo sbyoṅ rtsa
tshig. English. IV. Title.
BQ7670.6.G67 1998
294.3'444—dc21   98-14408

ISBN 0-86171-139-4

03 02 01 00 99
    6   5   4   3   2

Designed by: Gopa

Cover image: Shakyamuni Buddha with scenes of his
former lives. Photo by John Bigelow Taylor, N.Y.C.

Printed in the United States of America.

CONTENTS

PUBLISHER'S ACKNOWLEDGMENT

The publisher gratefully acknowledges the generous help of the Hershey Family Foundation in sponsoring the production of this book.

FOREWORD

To all of you who read this precious holy Dharma text, I would like to mention how extremely fortunate you are to have this opportunity to receive the precious holy teachings of guru Gomo Rinpoche, whose kindness is greater than that of all the past, present, and future buddhas.

Rinpoche once wrote me a letter from his home in Mussorie, India, telling me that he had hopes of definitely becoming enlightened in his very lifetime. This statement implies that Rinpoche's mind had become one with the practice; in other words, his mind had become one with guru devotion (the root of the path to enlightenment), as well as renunciation, the mind of enlightenment (*bodhichitta*), the wisdom realizing emptiness, and the two stages of tantra. It means that he had attained the realizations of clear light and illusory body because, without these realizations, he could not have said that he hoped to become enlightened in his lifetime.

In fact, it was obvious to us disciples that Rinpoche's teachings on tantra came from his own personal experience, and, in spite of our ordinary obscured way of perceiving things, we could still see that he had incredible qualities. As a result of his subdued mind and his realizations, his teachings immediately subdued the minds of his listeners. Just as snow naturally melts in the heat of the sun and butter melts on a hot pan, his teachings, due to his wisdom and compassion, naturally cooled, or pacified, our disturbed emotional minds.

The topic of the teachings contained in this book is mind training, or thought transformation, which is the most profound form of psychology and the best form of meditation. The teachings on mind training explain how to integrate our daily life experiences with meditation and Dharma practice, especially when we experience problems and our minds are filled with disturbing emotions. The mind training teachings show us how to make our lives beneficial even in times of difficulty by using problems as the path to enlightenment, the highest happiness. Through thought transformation practice—the application of either the ultimate mind of enlightenment, the realization of emptiness, or the conventional mind of enlightenment, the thought to achieve enlightenment for the benefit of all sentient beings—we can transform the experience of any difficulty (relationship problems, cancer, AIDS, and even our own death) into a cause for all sentient beings' happiness. In other words, not only do our sufferings become the cause of our own happiness, they also become the cause of countless other sentient beings' happiness. Through practicing mind training we can transform even the experience of problems into something extremely beneficial and useful for other sentient beings.

Mind training allows us to use problems as a method to purify our mental obscurations and the negative actions we committed in the past. Through developing the mind of enlightenment, we will also simultaneously accumulate merit similar in extent to the infinite sky. Thus, through the practice of transforming our minds, problems become a quick path to enlightenment.

Because Rinpoche himself lived the practice of mind training, his teachings come from experience and are not just empty words. For this reason, we are extremely fortunate to have this opportunity to study his teachings and to put into practice whatever we have understood.

I hope and pray that numberless sentient beings have the chance to read this book and thereby plant the seeds of liberation and enlightenment in their minds. May they achieve enlightenment as quickly as possible.

Lama Thubten Zopa Rinpoche
Kopan Monastery, Nepal
November 1995

EDITOR'S ACKNOWLEDGMENTS

I EXTEND MY HEARTFELT GRATITUDE to my spiritual guide and precious teacher Geshe Jampa Gyatso for his patient help in translating Gomo Rinpoche's *Annotations to the Root Verses of Mind Training*, which was at times difficult due to the use of a colloquial Tibetan largely unfamiliar to me.

Many thanks to Denis Huet, director of Institut Vajra Yogini, Lavaur, France, for his kind permission to include the oral commentary on *Annotations to the Root Verses of Mind Training* given by Gomo Tulku at this Foundation for the Preservation of the Mahayana Tradition (FPMT) center in April 1985.

I also extend my thanks to Dyanna Cridelich for her excellent work in transcribing the oral commentaries that form the basis of this book, and to John Dunne, of Wisdom Publications, for his invaluable editorial comments.

Lastly, I would also like to express my appreciation to Massimo Stordi (Gelong Thubten Tsognyi), a devoted disciple of both the late and present incarnation of Gomo Tulku, for asking me to work on preparing this text for publication, thus giving me a precious opportunity to study and reflect on the methods of mind training.

TECHNICAL NOTE

The text *Annotations to the Root Verses of Mind Training* by Gomo Tulku was translated on the basis of an earlier English translation by Thubten Jampa and George Churinoff (Gelong Thubten Tsultrim) and an Italian translation by Massimo Stordi (Gelong Thubten Tsognyi). The commentary included here was obtained by merging a brief teaching on this text given by Gomo Tulku in February 1985 at Istituto Lama Tzong Khapa, Pomaia, Italy, with a more extensive teaching given in April 1985 at Institut Vajra Yogini, Lavaur, France.

PREFACE

W HEN WE EXPERIENCE adversity, our tendency is to point to people and conditions external to ourselves as the source of all our problems. Consequently, during difficult periods in our lives we tend to find fault in whomever we meet, even in our friends and relatives. In contrast, when we apply specific methods for training the mind, we practice looking inside ourselves for the reasons we are experiencing hardship and adversity. As we do so, we will eventually discover that we alone are responsible for all our problems. This is because the real reason behind all our problems is that we have not been taking care of our own minds. Instead, we have allowed them to run wild, whereby they have become dominated by the three mental poisons of attachment, hatred, and ignorance. In fact, having carefully examined the source of our problems, we will conclude that not even one of them is caused by conditions external to our own mind. On further investigation, we will also realize that because of familiarity with the mental poisons during many past lives, we will continue to experience suffering in this and all our future lives if we do not take action against those poisons now.

The main reason we are still unable to take care of our minds and have not yet applied the antidotes, or remedies, to the three mental poisons is the strong tendency we have to cherish ourselves above others. This tendency shows itself in a variety of ways, such as cherishing our bodies and belongings. However, in my own experience, the most harmful of selfish attitudes is that of being happy and pleased with people who help or praise us and, on the other hand, being unhappy and angry with people who speak harshly to us or criticize us. These feelings, in turn, bring about attachment and anger toward these so-called friends and enemies. These negative emotions, the result of cherishing ourselves, totally destroy our mental happiness and bring about a state of confusion. On the contrary, if we are able to view other people and their actions with equanimity, we would discover real peace of mind.

Generally speaking, when other people treat us well—for example, in my own case when they show me respect or make offerings to me—we tend to feel very pleased and gratified. However, having practiced the methods for training the mind, I can honestly say that I no longer have these feelings. Now, even when people do not treat me with respect or do not help me, I manage to remain very relaxed and peaceful, without unhappy or negative thoughts in my mind. In fact, I have chosen to teach this particular topic, the practice of mind training, because I myself have personally experienced its great benefit. In 1948, I lived through a period of great hardship and difficulty. I was very unhappy, and my mind was filled with frustration and tension. In consequence, I began to look for some means to bring my mind back under control so as to regain a state of mental tranquility. In the end, I discovered that the only way to remain happy was to engage in the practices collectively known as *mind training*, in Tibetan *lo jong* (*blo sbyong*). I therefore read many texts on this subject and, at the same time, I tried to put these methods into practice. Through doing so, I eventually was able to bring my mind back under control and to regain inner peace and contentment. Then, to remind myself of the mind training practices, I wrote a commentary, based on my own experience, to Geshe Chekawa's mind training text *Seven Point Mind Training* (bLo sbyong don bdun ma).

As a refugee in India in 1962, I once again experienced a diffi-cult and unhappy period. As before, I turned to the practice of mind training and read many texts written on this subject by the great yogis of the past. At this time, I also rewrote my commen-tary on *Seven Point Mind Training*, the original having been lost when left behind in Tibet, which was subsequently checked and amended by the junior tutor of His Holiness the Dalai Lama, Kyabje Trijang Rinpoche.

May these teachings on mind training be of benefit whenever you too experience mental and physical problems.

Gomo Tulku
Istituto Lama Tzong Khapa
Pomaia, Italy
February 1985

THE ROOT VERSES
of
SEVEN POINT MIND TRAINING

---

by Geshe Chekawa

Homage to great compassion.

These instructions are the essence of the nectar.
They have been passed down from Serlingpa.
They are like a diamond, the sun, and a medicinal tree.
Understand the purpose and so forth of these texts.
When the five degenerations are flourishing,
  transform them into the path to enlightenment.

1 PRELIMINARY SUPPORTING DHARMA PRACTICES

Initially, train in the preliminaries.

2 TRAINING THE MIND IN THE PATH TO ENLIGHTENMENT

Put all the blame on the one.
Meditate on everyone as kind.
Train alternately in the two, taking and giving.
Begin taking with yourself.
Mount the two upon the breath.
There are three objects, three poisons,
  and three roots of virtue.

These, in brief, are the instructions
    for the post-meditation period.
Be mindful in order to admonish yourself.
Train yourself with the verses during
    all activities.
Having attained stability, be shown the secret.
Consider phenomena to be like a dream.
Analyze the nature of ungenerated awareness.
Even the antidote itself is naturally free.
Focus on the nature of the basis of all,
    the entity of the path.
Between sessions be an illusionist.

3 BRINGING UNFAVORABLE CONDITIONS INTO THE PATH TO ENLIGHTENMENT

When the vessel and its contents are filled
    with negativities,
Transform these unfavorable conditions
    into the path to enlightenment.
Immediately apply whatever you meet to meditation.
Possess the four preparations, the supreme method.

4 INTEGRATING THE PRACTICES IN A SINGLE LIFETIME

In brief, the essence of the instructions
    is to apply the five forces.
The Great Vehicle instructions on transference
    are those very five forces; cherish this behavior.

5 THE MEASURE OF A TRAINED MIND

Combine all the Dharma into one intention.
Of the two witnesses, rely on the primary one.
Always rely on mental happiness alone.
The measure of being trained is to
    no longer regress.
To be trained is to possess the five signs
    of greatness.
You are trained when able even if distracted.

Constantly train in the three general points.
Change your attitude, but remain natural.
Do not mention [others'] impaired limbs.
Do not think about others' affairs.
Initially, purify whatever affliction is the strongest.
Give up all hope of reward.
Avoid poisoned food.
Do not hold a grudge.
Do not respond to malicious talk.
Do not lie in ambush.
Do not strike to the core.
Do not put the load of a *dzo* on an ox.
Do not aim to win the race.
Do not use perverse means.
Do not turn a god into a demon.
Do not seek [others'] suffering as a means
   to your own happiness.

*The Root Verses
of Seven Point
Mind Training*

7 ADVICE REGARDING MIND TRAINING

Perform all yogas with the one.
Apply the one to all perverse oppressors.
Do the two activities, one at the beginning
   and one at the end.
Be patient whichever of the two occurs.
Guard the two at the risk of your life.
Train in the three difficult ones.
Obtain the three principal causes.
Cultivate the three without deterioration.
Possess the three without separation.
Train in purity and impartiality with respect
   to objects.
Cherish all of the encompassing and
   profound trainings.
Meditate constantly on the special cases.
Do not look for other conditions.
Practice the most important right now.
Avoid the distorted understandings.

Do not be erratic.
Train continuously.
Attain liberation with the two, investigation
    and analysis.
Do not boast.
Refrain from retaliating.
Do not act impetuously.
Do not wish for gratitude.

The cause being my strong admiration, I ignored suffering and a bad reputation and requested these instructions for subduing self-grasping. Now even when I die, I will have no regrets.

A   P R O L O G U E
to
M I N D   T R A I N I N G

INITIAL HOMAGE

Gomo Tulku's Homage

namo guruye

I bow to the Kinsman of the Sun who revealed the instructions for training in the mind of enlightenment. These instructions are the quintessence of the eighty-four thousand collections of Dharma that he himself, the Peerless Founder and Lord of the Ten Strengths, taught.

I begin the commentary to the *Root Verses of Mind Training* by paying homage, or bowing, to the holy being, Shakyamuni Buddha, whose poetic epithets include Kinsman of the Sun, Peerless Founder, and Lord of the Ten Strengths. The very essence of the eighty-four thousand collections of teachings that he taught as the antidotes to the eighty-four thousand afflictions is the mind of enlightenment, the altruistic aspiration to attain enlightenment for the benefit of all sentient beings.

> With heartfelt great respect, I bow with my three doors to the direct and lineage holy beings, Serlingpa, Dipamkara, and the rest, who came one after the other, the

5

source of these precious instructions on training the mind as taught by [the Buddha].

I pay homage to the direct and lineage gurus of the transmission of the instructions for generating the mind of enlightenment. These teachings were passed down through Dharmakirti of Indonesia, known as Serlingpa in Tibetan (lit., "One from the Golden Isle"), to his Indian disciple Atisha (982– 1054), who is also known as Dipamkara Shrijñana. Atisha, in turn, transmitted them to his foremost Tibetan disciple, Dromtönpa (1005–64), who then passed them on to the Kadam geshe Potowa (1031–1106). Geshe Potowa transmitted them to his disciple Geshe Sharawa (1070–1141), who subsequently passed them on to Geshe Chekawa (1101–1175). This master put the mind training teachings into practice and summarized them in seven points in his text *Seven Point Mind Training.* He did so to simplify the mind training teachings and thereby make it easier for others to practice them. Geshe Chekawa wrote *Seven Point Mind Training* in prose form and only later, some time in the early nineteenth century, was it versified by Keutsang Jamyang Monlam Rinpoche; he called the resultant text *Root Verses of Seven Point Mind Training* (bLo sby-ong rtsa tshig).

The mind training teachings were transmitted in an unbroken lineage from Geshe Chekawa to Pabongka Rinpoche, from whom I personally received the transmission of these teachings. The mere fact that these teachings have been transmitted in an unbroken lineage from teacher to disciple makes them of great benefit to a practitioner's mind, but this is not the only reason for their benefit; in addition, they were listened to, put into practice, and realized by the gurus of the past.

Having expressed this homage, I will now discuss the *Root Verses [of Seven Point Mind Training].*

There are a great variety of mind training texts, some of which are very detailed and extensive while others of which are very brief and concise. However, all of these texts share the same purpose. Each one was written to show how to train the mind to attain enlightenment for the benefit of all sentient beings.

GESHE CHEKAWA'S HOMAGE

Homage to great compassion.

This [line] expresses homage to great mercy-compassion, the principal topic of this text.

Geshe Chekawa, the author of *Seven Point Mind Training,* pays homage to the actual topic of his text, the great compassion present in the mental continua of all the buddhas.

THE ESSENCE OF
THE BUDDHA'S TEACHINGS

These instructions are the essence of the nectar.

[Buddha's] teachings destroy the sufferings, such as birth, aging, sickness, and death, produced by the eighty-four thousand afflictions. In addition, they easily bestow non-abiding nirvana. These instructions are the essence, or nectar, of these teachings. In other words, they are the quintessence of the eighty-four thousand collections of Dharma.

As I have mentioned, Buddha taught eighty-four thousand collections of Dharma as antidotes to the eighty-four thousand afflictions that generate every type of suffering, including the human sufferings of birth, aging, sickness, and death. The mind of enlightenment is the actual antidote that destroys the eighty-four thousand afflictions. When the eighty-four thousand teachings are condensed, their very essence is found to be the mind training practices, which are engaged in for the purpose of developing the mind of enlightenment.

The principal cause for achieving the state of buddhahood is the mind of enlightenment, while the principal cause for achieving liberation from cyclic existence is the realization of emptiness. Wisdom, the realization of emptiness, without method, the mind of enlightenment, is said to be bondage, while the realization of emptiness together with the mind of enlightenment is said to be liberation. The reason for this is that after one has realized emptiness, if that realization is not sustained by the mind of enlightenment, one merely will achieve the personal peace of nirvana.

In this state of nirvana one neglects all other suffering sentient beings; therefore, it is considered to be a type of bondage. For example, although hearer and solitary realizer foe destroyers have attained the direct realization of emptiness and the state of nirvana, they lack great compassion; hence, they are unable to achieve the state of enlightenment. On the other hand, when the realization of emptiness is sustained by great compassion, it results in great liberation, the state of buddhahood. On the other hand, if one possesses the mind of enlightenment but lacks the realization of emptiness, this too is bondage because one remains bound by the mental afflictions in the prison of cyclic existence. In short, to achieve the state of perfectly complete enlightenment, it is essential to unify the practices of method and wisdom.

THE MIND TRAINING LINEAGE

They have been passed down from Serlingpa.

These instructions belong to guru Atisha and combine the lineages of guru Dharmarakshita, guru Maitriyogi, and guru Serlingpa into one stream. Moreover, they constitute the tradition of Kadam geshe Chekawa's *Seven Point Mind Training.*

The Indian masters Atisha (982–1054) and Shantideva (c. 700) are the sources of two well-known mind training techniques for developing the mind of enlightenment. The mind training practice that descends from Atisha is commonly known as the *sevenfold causes and effect,* while that which descends from Shantideva is known as *equalizing and exchanging oneself with others.*

Atisha himself received the transmission of the lineages of the teachings on mind training from three principal gurus, Dharmarakshita, Maitriyogi, and Serlingpa. However, the particular mind training instructions included in the *Seven Point Mind Training* originate from Atisha's Indonesian guru, Serlingpa. Atisha, having heard that it was possible to receive instructions from this master on how to develop the mind of enlightenment, set off on a long and dangerous sea voyage to Indonesia. The journey took seven months, and among the many difficulties encountered was a huge storm that threatened to destroy the ship. However, as a result of Atisha's fervent prayers, the twenty-one Taras appeared during the storm and protected the ship from harm.

On his arrival, Atisha received the instructions for developing the mind of enlightenment from Serlingpa. These are the very means by which one can attain enlightenment. For this reason, Atisha, in spite of having had many other gurus, always considered Serlingpa to be his crown ornament.

Years later, Atisha was invited to Tibet where he devoted the latter part of his life to the propagation and preservation of Buddhism in this country. Here he transmitted the instructions on the mind of enlightenment to his foremost disciple Dromtönpa, through whom they have been passed down in an unbroken lineage to our present-day teachers.

ANALOGIES OF THE MIND TRAINING INSTRUCTIONS

They are like a diamond, the sun,
and a medicinal tree.

Just as a precious diamond, even broken, still outshines all the finest jewelry, likewise, those who possess merely a part of the instructions on the precious mind of enlightenment outshine all the hearer and solitary realizer foe destroyers. And just as the rays of the sun, even when it is rising, dispel the darkness [of the night], likewise, the mere possession of the instructions for training in the mind of enlightenment dispels the darkness of self-grasping and ignorance. And just as the mere branches and leaves of a medicinal tree are able to eliminate the four hundred diseases, likewise, a mere part of the instructions for training in the mind of enlightenment is able to eliminate the chronic disease of the eighty-four thousand afflictions.

The usefulness and value of the instructions for training in the mind of enlightenment are demonstrated by way of three analogies that compare them to a diamond, the sun, and a medicinal tree.

1. Just as even a tiny fragment of a diamond outshines all other precious jewels, likewise, those who possess even a tiny part of

the instructions on the conventional mind of enlightenment outshine all others, even the hearers and solitary realizers.

2. Just as the rising sun naturally dispels the darkness, likewise, the possession of the instructions for training in the ultimate mind of enlightenment naturally dispels the darkness of ignorance.

3. Just as even a part of a medicinal tree is able to cure disease, likewise, even a part of the instructions for training in the mind of enlightenment is able to eliminate the disease that afflicts our mental continua, the eighty-four thousand afflictions.

THE TOPIC OF THE
MIND TRAINING TEXTS

Understand the purpose and so forth of these texts.

The main purpose of these texts is to explain the instructions for training in the mind of enlightenment.[1]

The topic of all the mind training texts is the instructions for developing the conventional and ultimate minds of enlightenment. Geshe Chekawa mentions this here to emphasize the fact that, although there are many texts on mind training, their main purpose is the same in that they all explain the practices for training in the mind of enlightenment.

TRANSFORMING UNFAVORABLE
CONDITIONS INTO THE PATH

*When the five degenerations are flourishing,
transform them into the path to enlightenment.*

The five degenerations concern (1) time, (2) sentient beings, (3) afflictions, (4) life span, and (5) views. These five are presently on the increase and there are few conditions for happiness, much harm from humans and non-humans, and many occasions for contending with negative conditions. It is at this time that you should transform such unfavorable conditions into the path to enlightenment.

Because we live in a period in which the five degenerations are flourishing, we are forced to experience many types of adverse conditions, such as those caused by human beings and other types of beings. At the same time, good conditions are increasingly rare, such that even when we try to do something positive we often encounter difficulties and tend to meet with little success. For these reasons it is extremely important for us to transform all such adverse conditions into the path to enlightenment by applying the mind training practices.

A Prologue to Mind Training

· I ·

PRELIMINARY SUPPORTING
DHARMA PRACTICES

Initially, train in the preliminaries.

Train your mind in the stages of the path of an inferior
being through reflecting on:

1. the freedoms and endowments,
2. their great meaning,
3. the difficulty of obtaining them,
4. death-impermanence,
5. the fact that nothing other than Dharma
   is of benefit at the time of death,
6. the sufferings of the three unfortunate migrations,
7. going for refuge,
8. actions and their results.

Then, train your mind well in the stages of the path of a
middling being through reflecting on such sufferings as:

1. the faults of cyclic existence:
   a. uncertainty with respect to one's
      enemies and friends,
   b. dissatisfaction,
   c. repeated loss of one's body,
   d. repeated rebirth,
   e. incessant loss of high status,
   f. separation from one's friends and relatives;

2. [the general sufferings of cyclic existence]:
    a. suffering of change,
    b. suffering of suffering,
    c. pervasive compositional suffering;

3. [the specific sufferings of the upper realms]:
    a. of human beings: birth, aging, sickness,
        and death,
    b. of the gods: a long life,
    c. of the demigods: jealousy.

The preliminary practices consist of the various meditations intended for inferior and middling practitioners. These preliminaries support the main practice of superior practitioners, the training in the mind of enlightenment. Practitioners of mind training should begin by familiarizing themselves with these lower meditations prior to engaging in the actual mind training practices.

The practices of an inferior being, a Dharma practitioner of inferior scope, include meditations on such topics as guru devotion, the great meaning of a precious human rebirth with the freedoms and endowments, death-impermanence, and so forth. Having trained well in these meditations, practitioners subsequently then begin to train in the practices of a middling being, a Dharma practitioner of middle scope, through meditating on such topics as the faults of cyclic existence, the general and specific sufferings of cyclic existence, and so forth.

DHARMA PRACTITIONERS
OF THE INFERIOR SCOPE

Inferior beings, or Dharma practitioners of inferior scope, are so called because their motivation for engaging in spiritual practices is merely to achieve their own happiness in future lives through avoiding rebirth in the three lower realms. Practitioners of inferior scope meditate on six main topics:

1. guru devotion,
2. the meaningfulness and difficulty
    of obtaining a precious human rebirth,
3. death-impermanence,
4. the sufferings of the lower realms,

5. going for refuge,
6. actions and their results.

1. Guru Devotion

In general, there are two types of Dharma practitioners. The first are people of lesser intelligence who are called *followers of faith.* When such people hear that a well-known teacher is scheduled to give teachings, they rush to listen to him or her without first examining the qualities of that teacher. The second type of Dharma practitioners are those of greater intelligence who are called *followers of reasoning.* These people take the time to investigate the qualities of a particular teacher, and seek to determine whether that teacher actually puts the Dharma teachings into practice. Only after having ascertained that a particular teacher is well qualified does a follower of reasoning then put faith in that teacher as a guru. When this kind of preliminary examination is done, a disciple's guru devotion is stable, and he or she runs no risk that it will deteriorate.

If, after examining a particular teacher, we find him or her to be qualified, we should follow the advice of the old Tibetan saying, "Act like a blind man holding the tail of a cow." Once a blind person has taken hold of the tail of a cow to follow a path, he cannot risk letting go. On the other hand, if he holds tightly and resolutely to the tail of the cow, he will safely reach his destination. Likewise, to achieve success in our spiritual practice, it is crucial for us to be extremely stable and consistent in our devotion to our guru; we should not change gurus for any reason. If we behave in this way, we will definitely be able to achieve realizations even in the very short lifetime of these degenerate times.

The meditation on guru devotion is divided into four topics:

a. guru devotion by means of thought,
b. guru devotion by means of action,
c. the advantages of correct guru devotion,
d. the disadvantages of improper guru devotion.

a. Guru devotion by means of thought

The main reason I have been able to bring about a change in my mind, to be consistent in the practice of mind training, and to generate positive states of mind is the kindness of my gurus—from my first guru who taught me the alphabet up to my last guru who taught me the most profound teachings. In fact, any beneficial result that I have experienced from the mind training practices is due mainly to the blessings I received from my gurus.

To demonstrate the importance of guru devotion an anecdote is often recounted from the life of the Indian master Atisha, who spent the last seventeen years of his life teaching in Tibet. Atisha was once questioned as to the reason why none of the many meditators in Tibet had gained any spiritual realizations. Atisha responded that it was because Tibetans tend to think of their gurus as ordinary beings. I have met many people over the years who have told me that, in spite of their having practiced Dharma for quite some time, they still had not gained any realizations; from my side, I think the reason is a lack of guru devotion.

To develop guru devotion, the essence of which is to see the guru as an actual buddha, we can rely on valid scriptures. For example, there is a frequently cited tantric passage in which Vajradhara explicitly states that the guru is actually a buddha. This statement is considered to be valid because the conqueror Vajradhara is the founder of the whole tantric path. As such, this citation is considered sufficient evidence for establishing that the guru is indeed a buddha; one need not present any other evidence. However, to develop further conviction that the guru is indeed a buddha, we also can rely on quotations from such valid scriptures as Maitreya's *Ornament for Clear Realization* (Abhisamayālaṃkāra, mNgon par rtogs pa'i rgyan). In the eighth chapter of this particular text there are several verses that have personally inspired me very much and helped me develop faith that the guru is an actual manifestation of a buddha. Two such verses are "As long as existence lasts, [the buddhas] will benefit migrating beings in various ways" and "Likewise, their actions are asserted to continue without interruption as long as cyclic existence lasts." With these verses Maitreya states that buddhas will appear in the future in a variety of ways to teach beings of different levels and capacities. Buddhas use this approach because it would be extremely difficult for ordinary sentient beings to perceive them if they were to appear manifestly in their actual form as buddhas. Also, as Pabongka Rinpoche tells us in *Liberation in the Palm of Your Hand*, we are very fortunate that in spite of our mental obscurations we are able to see our guru in a human form and not, for example, as an animal. In other words, if we were to have even more karmic obscurations, we would not be able to see the guru as a human being; instead, we would perceive him perhaps in the form of a horse, a dog, or a donkey!

To illustrate how fortunate we are in this regard, we can recall a story of an event that happened not long ago; it concerns a certain Kagyu lama named Losang Tönden. It is said that one day, when this particular lama was giving teachings near Drepung Monastery, among the thousands of people listening to him was a monk who was unable to see or hear him teaching; instead, the monk perceived him to be sitting on the throne eating meat. This story illustrates how people perceive the same guru in different ways according to their karmic obscurations. To avoid having such distorted perceptions in the future, it is important for us to practice seeing all the actions of the guru as wholesome and meaningful and to make prayers to always be able to see the guru in a human form.

Through thinking about the qualities and kindness of our gurus we will develop deep faith in and respect for them and consequently correctly devote ourselves to them by means of thought.

b. Guru devotion by means of action

Guru devotion by means of action involves the performance of physical actions, such as rendering service to the guru by helping him in whatever way is needed, making offerings to him, and generally engaging in actions that please him. In my own case, all my gurus were extremely good and kind to me, and I always tried to practice very pure devotion toward them. I expressed my devotion by, for example, taking exceptional care of their belongings, never gossiping about other people with them, and even avoiding walking on their shadows.

c. The advantages of correct guru devotion

One of the benefits of guru devotion is that due to having pure faith in a teacher, we will be able to understand quickly whatever he or she teaches and to apply it directly to our spiritual practice. By practicing pure guru devotion we will be able eventually to have as many as a thousand gurus without committing any faults in our devotion. Without pure guru devotion, even if we listen to the teachings of a very highly qualified guru they will benefit our minds little.

In short, the advantages of practicing guru devotion correctly by means of thought and action are that we will please our guru and, consequently, all the buddhas will respond by granting us their blessings through the guru.

d. The disadvantages of improper guru devotion

One time the Buddha was questioned about the disadvantages of improper guru devotion. Although his reply was very lengthy, in essence he responded that the consequence is rebirth in the lower realms. This result is more specifically mentioned in a citation in *Liberation in the Palm of Your Hand* that says: as a result of improper guru devotion, one will be reborn as a dog a hundred times and then as a human being of bad caste. Due to these and other disadvantages, we should take great care not to engage in actions that would be improper in terms of our devotion to our guru.

In short, since the success of the mind training practices is dependent on a firm foundation of pure guru devotion, I emphasize the need to practice it right from the very beginning of one's spiritual practice. However, although this is my advice, I am merely presenting this topic to you; it is up to you to make your own decision as to whether you wish to practice guru devotion.

Furthermore, although sincere guru devotion is definitely necessary on the part of the disciples, the guru should not have any expectations from his disciples. In *Stages on the Path*, Lama Tsongkhapa warns us about this. He notes that if a guru becomes extremely unhappy when his disciples make a small mistake and becomes excessively pleased when they make him an offering, it is a sign that this particular guru is not qualified to lead them on the path to enlightenment.

2. Precious Human Rebirth

Having engaged in the practice of guru devotion for a long time, we should begin to meditate on the value of this precious human rebirth and the difficulty of obtaining such a rebirth again. A precious human rebirth is characterized by eight freedoms and ten endowments. The eight freedoms are:

a. one has not been born as a hell being;
b. one has not been born as an animal;
c. one has not been born as a hungry ghost;
d. one has not been born as a long-life god;
e. one has not been born in a barbaric country;
f. one has not been born with impaired mental
   or sense faculties, such as being deaf and dumb;
g. one does not hold wrong views;
h. one has not been born in a period in which
   a buddha did not teach.

If we have these freedoms, we have the freedom and the opportunity to practice Dharma. On the other hand, if we are born in a situation that lacks any one of these freedoms, we do not have the opportunity to practice Dharma. Only those human beings who have these freedoms — and therefore the conditions necessary to be able to practice Dharma — are said to have a precious human rebirth. In this way a precious human rebirth should not be confused with just any human rebirth. This is amply illustrated by an event that occurred in Tibet. One day Purchog Ngawang Jampa was giving a teaching on the precious human rebirth, its freedoms and endowments, and the difficulty of obtaining such a rebirth. Among the many people listening to this teaching was a Chinese man who voiced his objection to Purchog Ngawang Jampa, saying, "Surely you have not visited China, for if you had, you would have definitely seen the enormous number of Chinese and have understood that a human rebirth is not so difficult to obtain at all!"

In addition to the eight freedoms, the perfect human rebirth also has ten endowments that are subdivided into five personal and five circumstantial endowments. The five personal endowments are:

a. one has been born as a human being;
b. one has born in a central, or spiritual, country;
c. one possesses unimpaired mental and sense faculties;
d. one has not committed any of the five
   actions of immediate retribution;
e. one has faith in the Three Jewels.

The five circumstantial endowments are:

a. a buddha has come to this world;
b. a buddha has turned the wheel of Dharma;
c. a buddha's teachings are still extant;
d. there are ordained people;
e. there are people who have love and
   compassion for Dharma practitioners.

Having obtained a perfect human rebirth, it is essential to take advantage of this great fortune, for if we do not, we will squander this rare opportunity. We would be acting like someone who, having set out to obtain precious jewels, arrives at a place full of them, but returns empty-handed. To illustrate how important it is to take advantage of this precious human rebirth, we can recall a tale recounted in *The Essential Nectar.* Once upon a time, there was an old blind man. One day, while walking on a hillside, he fell over a ledge and landed on the back of a wild ass. The ass, who had never before allowed anyone to ride him, began to run very fast. The old man held very tightly to the ass's mane, but the tighter he held, the faster the ass ran. Eventually, they burst into a busy marketplace. Many people saw the old blind man clinging to the ass and wondered what had happened. The blind man pretended that he was purposely sitting on the ass and began to sing. When asked what he was doing, he replied, "If I do not sing today, when should I sing?" This story tells us that, like the blind man enjoying the rare opportunity of riding a wild ass, it is extremely important, while we still have the chance, to make use in a meaningful way of this perfect human body, so rare and precious.

3. Death-Impermanence

Although we have this precious human rebirth now, the time of our death is completely uncertain, and the life span of human beings in general is highly variable. This variability is indicated by the scriptures which say that, although human beings once had a life span of eighty-thousand years, it gradually decreased to the present maximum of about a hundred years. As for the uncertainty of when death will come, the teachings on the stages of the path remind us that we do not know which will come first: tomorrow morning or our next rebirth. By emphasizing the uncertainty of death in this way, these teachings urge us to practice Dharma right now.

Through reflecting on the fragility of this perfect human rebirth and the fact that death is certain to happen to us all, we come to a strong determination to practice Dharma right now because only our practice can help us at the time of death. Having practiced Dharma in this life, we will die without fear, and our rebirth will be good. However, if we do not practice Dharma during our lifetime, we will die depressed and afraid, and then take rebirth in the lower realms, where we will experience much suffering.

4. The Sufferings of the Lower Realms

Next, as a further impetus for us to engage in spiritual practice without delay, we meditate on the sufferings of the beings in the three lower realms: the hell beings, hungry ghosts, and animals. In this context, we reflect on the sufferings of extreme heat and cold of the beings born in the two main hell realms, the sufferings of hunger and thirst of the hungry ghosts, and the sufferings of the animals who live in the ocean (said to be countless in number and crowded together) and those scattered throughout the realms of gods and humans.

5. Going for Refuge

Then, to ensure that we are not reborn in the lower realms, we meditate on the qualities of the Three Jewels—the Buddha, Dharma, and Sangha—and go for refuge to them from the depths of our hearts.

6. Actions and Their Results

Whether going for refuge to the Three Jewels will be much help to us depends very much on our behavior. It is our own negative actions that lead us to the lower realms, so in addition to going for refuge to the Three Jewels, we also have to be extremely careful not to commit even the slightest negative action. When, however, we do mistakenly commit a nonvirtuous action, even a

small one, we should not disregard it; instead we should immediately purify it because, by their nature, actions increase in
strength exponentially. For example, if we were to kill an insect
today and not confess it, this negative action would continue to
increase in strength day by day. A good understanding of the
law of actions and results—that unwholesome actions lead to
suffering and wholesome actions to happiness and so forth—is
absolutely essential for a mind training practitioner because
morality is the very basis of mind training.

DHARMA PRACTITIONERS
OF THE MIDDLING SCOPE

Middling beings, Dharma practitioners of middling scope, are
not only motivated by a desire to avoid rebirth in the three lower
realms; they also seek to achieve their complete liberation from
the entirety of cyclic existence. However, although this attitude is
superior to that of an inferior being, it is still inferior to the attitude
of superior beings. Superior beings wish not only to eliminate the
causes of suffering, the mental afflictions, from their own mental
continua but also strive to attain enlightenment to help all other
sentient beings attain liberation from cyclic existence.

As practitioners of middling scope, we need to meditate on the
various sufferings of cyclic existence (which are summarized in
six faults and three general sufferings). We do so to gain a deep
and clear understanding that even rebirth in the three upper
realms—whether as a god, demigod, or human—is still by
nature suffering. In addition, we need to meditate on the specific
sufferings that characterize each of these realms. For example,
human beings experience eight specific types of suffering. They
are born; they fall sick; they age; they die; they are deprived of
pleasant objects; they encounter unpleasant objects; they fail to
obtain what they seek; and finally, they possess a human body
which by its very nature is suffering.

As for the gods, they experience three specific types of suffering: the suffering of having a long life span, the suffering of once
again falling into the lower realms, and the suffering of experiencing the signs of death. The specific suffering of the demigods
is that they continually, yet always unsuccessfully, engage in bat-
tle with the gods due to their intense jealousy.

In short, even if we take rebirth in one of the upper realms as a human, demigod, or god, we unavoidably experience the general sufferings of cyclic existence as well as the sufferings specific to that realm.

Preliminary
Supporting
Dharma
Practices

· 2 ·

TRAINING THE MIND

in the

PATH TO ENLIGHTENMENT

THE CONVENTIONAL MIND
OF ENLIGHTENMENT

> *Put all the blame on the one.*

> Other than your own self-grasping and self-cherishing,
> there is no one else whatsoever, either human or non-
> human, on whom to put the blame [for your unhap-
> piness]. The self-cherishing that is induced by the
> ignorance in your continua ignores the distinction
> between virtue and negativity and causes you to be
> jealous of your superiors, scorn your inferiors, and
> compete with your peers. When you understand that,
> from beginningless cyclic existence up to now, the sole
> instigator of your misery has been this very [attitude],
> you will enter the community of Dharma practitioners.
> Therefore, put the blame on [self-cherishing].

We should put the blame for all our problems on one source
alone: our self-cherishing attitude. Self-cherishing is the one to
blame because it causes us to ignore the law of actions and their
results, whereby we engage in negative actions that bring the
result of suffering rebirths and unpleasant experiences.

In our everyday life, when we are involved in difficult situations we tend to rationalize them by thinking, "I am not the cause of such and such a problem." We point our fingers at others and say, "They are the ones to blame." However, when we practice mind training we should stop thinking in this way. Instead, we should try to understand that every unpleasant experience arises from the selfish attitude of cherishing ourselves more than others. We should also constantly remember that the various types of unpleasant rebirths are not allotted to us by some higher being to punish us. Instead, those rebirths and the suffering they entail are caused by our own self-cherishing mind.

The basic error that underlies all our unpleasant experiences is the mental factor ignorance. It functions as the basis for the self-cherishing attitude that leads us to commit negative actions, to be jealous of people who are superior to us, to be arrogant and haughty toward people whom we consider inferior, and to compete with people who are our equals.

In short, we need to understand clearly that all the different problems and sufferings that we experience are caused by our own self-cherishing mind. For this reason the Kadam geshes used to call the self-cherishing mind "the owl-headed augur of bad omens." In the end, whether we are good Dharma practitioners is determined by how much we cherish ourselves.

Meditate on everyone as kind.

Every happiness and virtue in our continua comes about through other sentient beings; therefore, meditate in general on the kindness of sentient beings, your former mothers,[2] and meditate in particular on the kindness of harmful beings, both the human and non-human. When you experience any undesired harm, even something as minor as, for example, the bite of a fly or an ant, think: "Since beginningless time I have eaten this being's flesh and drunk its blood. This bite is payment for that karmic debt." In this way abandon any harmful intent toward their continua. And then, since the time has come to pay back these debts, pray to purify that karmic debt and then transform the undesired harm into an aid for generating the precious mind of enlightenment. Apply methods, or at the very least make fervent prayers, for the precious mind of enlightenment to be generated even in the continua of harmful sentient beings. As Langri Tangpa said, "Although I have opened and looked at many profound Dharma [texts], all mistakes are my own, while all good qualities belong to noble sentient beings. The essential point of this is to give the profit and victory to others and to take the loss and defeat upon oneself." He also said, "There is nothing other than this to understand."

Whatever happiness we experience comes about either directly or indirectly through the kindness of other sentient beings. Even the beings who harm us are actually very kind and helpful to us because they provide us with an opportunity to train in generating the mind of enlightenment. For this reason, we need to meditate on the kindness of all sentient beings without exception.

Whenever we experience mental or physical problems, whether big or small, we should reflect that they are the result of our own past actions. Even when we are bitten by a fly or an ant, we should not get angry and think to kill it; instead, we should reflect that the reason for this suffering is that at some time in the past we drank its blood and ate its flesh. By thinking in this way, we will feel happy that we now have the opportunity to repay this debt created in a previous life. Likewise, when a human being threatens or beats us or a particular spirit causes us to become sick, instead of generating hatred toward these beings, it would be much better to transform these adverse conditions into a method for generating the mind of enlightenment. To do so we can reflect, as Langri Tangpa said, that all our positive qualities come from other sentient beings, while all our negativities arise from our own side; hence, it is right to give the victory to others and take the defeat upon ourselves. We can also make prayers thinking, "May all the sentient beings who harm me quickly develop the mind of enlightenment."

Train alternately in the two, taking and giving.

By equalizing and exchanging yourself and others, train alternately [in taking and giving]. Visualize yourself as able to give your happiness and virtue to other sentient beings, and as able to take upon yourself the negativities and sufferings of other sentient beings. As it says in

Rays of Sunlight Mind Training, "Presently, other than merely contemplating taking and giving, it is difficult to actually take. However, having trained and familiarized yourself [with this practice], it will not be difficult to actually take. Therefore, train your mind."³

We need to train in the meditation of taking and giving in which we take upon ourselves all the negativities, sufferings, and so forth of other sentient beings and give them all our happiness, roots of virtue, and so forth. In connection with the practice of taking and giving, *Rays of Sunlight Mind Training* says that, although at the beginning it might be difficult to train in taking and giving, eventually through training ourselves well we will be able to actually take upon ourselves the suffering of others.

Begin taking with yourself.

When your intention to take the sufferings of others upon yourself is weak, initially develop mental strength through skillfully training as follows: in the morning, take upon yourself the suffering that you yourself will experience in the evening; then take upon yourself now the suffering that you will experience next year or in future rebirths, and so on.

If we are unable to take even our own problems upon ourselves, obviously we will be unable to take others' sufferings. Therefore, when we practice taking, we should begin with taking our own future sufferings upon ourselves right now. We can begin by taking upon ourselves right now the problems that we will experience later on today and tomorrow. Next we can gradually take upon ourselves this week the problems that we will experience next week. Then we can take upon ourselves this year the problems that we will experience next year, and so on. We continue in this way until we are able to take upon ourselves in this very life even the problems we will experience in future lives. Through training gradually like this, eventually we also will be able to take others' sufferings upon ourselves.

Mount the two upon the breath.

During the post-meditation period, while exhaling through your right nostril, give all your roots of virtue of the three times to all sentient beings, your former mothers. Imagine that thereby they all obtain uncontaminated happiness. Then, while inhaling through your left nostril, take upon yourself all the negativities and sufferings of all sentient beings, your former mothers, and imagine that they all become free from suffering.

You should perform "the two," taking and giving, in conjunction with the inhalation and exhalation of the breath. While exhaling through your right nostril, visualize giving your happiness, wealth, and roots of virtue of the three times (past, present, and future), in the form of white light, to all sentient beings. While inhaling through your left nostril, visualize taking upon yourself all their negative actions, suffering, and so forth in the form of black smoke. In addition, think that all the sufferings that other sentient beings will experience in the future are experienced by you right now, whereby they become completely free even from suffering in the future.

> *There are three objects, three poisons, and three roots of virtue.*

> The three objects are enemies, friends, and strangers; the three poisons are attachment, hatred, and ignorance; and the three roots of virtue are any virtuous practices that are not mixed with attachment, hatred, and ignorance.

The three objects are the three types of people, namely those whom we categorize as friends, enemies, and strangers. The three poisons are attachment, hatred, and ignorance, which arise in relation to the three objects, respectively. In other words, we feel attachment for our friends, hatred for our enemies, and indifference for strangers. The three roots of virtue are those virtuous practices that are not mixed with attachment, hatred, or ignorance. Therefore, for any action to be virtuous, including that of dedicating our merit to achieve enlightenment, our minds must be free from these three mental poisons.

> *These, in brief, are the instructions for the post-meditation period.*

> In brief, the instructions are to exchange the position of oneself and others through giving our virtues to sentient beings and taking their sufferings upon ourselves.

All the instructions can be synthesized into the mind training practice of giving our happiness to others and taking their suffering upon ourselves.

Be mindful in order to admonish yourself.

Admonish yourself by being ever mindful of whether or not your mind is contradicting the mind training [practices] of the Great Vehicle.

We need to be constantly mindful of whether we are contradicting or practicing the mind training practices of the Great Vehicle. In this way, when we catch ourselves doing something that is contrary to them, we will be able to stop immediately. For this reason, the mental factor mindfulness should always be present during all our activities.

Train with the verses during all activities.

Do not allow your mind to become separated from mind training during any activity whatsoever—including walking, standing, lying, and sitting—and verbally recite verses of mind training.

We need to train ourselves constantly in virtue by not allowing our minds to become separated from mind training and by reciting verses of mind training during all our activities, whether we are walking, standing, lying down, or sitting. For example, we can recite a mind training text when we are out walking, as this will prevent us from committing negativities. One mind training text that is ideal for this purpose because it is both short and easy to memorize is the *Eight Verses on Mind Training* by Langri Tangpa. Through reciting such verses of mind training, we will constantly remind ourselves of the mind training practices that we wish to avoid transgressing.

THE ULTIMATE MIND
OF ENLIGHTENMENT

Having attained stability, be shown the secret.

First, train your mind well in the precious mind of
enlightenment that forms part of method. Then, when
your familiarity with it is extremely stable, train next in
the precious ultimate mind of enlightenment, the wisdom that is inseparable from emptiness.

Having developed the conventional mind of enlightenment and
gained some stability in it, we should learn the secret, the meaning of emptiness, and then meditate on it until we realize it. By
practicing in this way, we eventually will achieve the unification
of the conventional mind of enlightenment and the realization
of emptiness, the ultimate mind of enlightenment.

Consider phenomena to be like a dream.

Reflect on the fact that the functioning things categorized as external objects (also called *apprehendeds* or *that
which is apprehended*) are dream-like because, except
for merely appearing to the mind as such, they do not
have even an iota of true existence.

Reflect that all external objects, both the environment and sentient beings, are like dreams in that they appear but do not exist
from their own side; in fact, they do not have even the least bit
of true existence. However, even though all phenomena are
merely labeled, or imputed, by the mind, they appear to us to be
truly existent. It is the basis of this appearance that we believe
they actually do exist in this way.

Analyze the nature of ungenerated awareness.

Reflect on the fact that the phenomena categorized as
inner subjects (also called *apprehenders* or *that which
apprehends*) are merely posited in dependence on the
gathering, or assembling, of their many respective causes and conditions; they do not apprehend, engage, or
act upon objects. Therefore, they do not have even an
iota of inherent existence.

Also reflect that the phenomena categorized as inner subjects, minds and mental factors, are like dreams in that they are not generated from their own side, but are merely imputed by thought.

In short, both objects (external phenomena) and subjects (inner phenomena) are like dreams.

> *Even the antidote itself is naturally free.*

Then, ascertain that not only are those phenomena categorized as external objects (apprehendeds) and inner subjects (apprehenders) not truly existent, but even suchness itself does not truly exist.

External objects, inner subjects, and even emptiness itself are not truly existent.

> *Focus on the nature of the basis of all, the entity*
> *of the path.*

In purely etymological terms, *basis of all* refers to the basis on which uncontaminated imprints are deposited. However, here [the basis of all refers to emptiness], which is the basis of all cyclic existence and nirvana. This is because when we realize emptiness, we will be able to attain the state of nirvana, but, as long as we do not realize it, we will not be able to put an end to cyclic existence. Moreover, since any dependently arising [phenomena] appears from emptiness, emptiness is like the basis for the arising of all such dependent relations of cyclic existence and nirvana. We should therefore cultivate the virtuous practice of meditative equipoise on the nature of emptiness.

The Chittamatra school of Buddhist tenets asserts an eighth consciousness, called the *basis of all*, that functions as a basis upon which uncontaminated imprints are deposited. However, the Prasangika Madhyamika school does not accept the existence of such a consciousness; instead, the Prasangikas assert that the *basis of all* is emptiness, the direct realization of which is essential for achieving nirvana. Because we are unable to achieve liberation from cyclic existence without the realization of emptiness, we should deepen our meditation on emptiness.

Between sessions be an illusionist.

Between meditation sessions, practice the "subsequent attainment" of illusory-like appearance, which is that all conventional phenomena appear, even though they are empty. Reflect as follows: to spectators, whose eyes have been affected by mantras and magic substances, pebbles, sticks, and such appear to be horses and oxen. Nevertheless, those pebbles, sticks, and so forth are not established to be actual horses and oxen. Similarly, other than merely appearing as such due to the influence of pollution from the imprints of ignorance, all conventional phenomena are not truly established.

During meditation sessions we focus our minds on emptiness. Then, in the subsequent attainment period, which is the interval between sessions, we should consider all external phenomena to be like an illusion conjured up by a magician. In other words, we should reflect that although the objects we perceive, such as trees and houses, appear to truly exist, they do not actually exist in this way. Illusions that have been created by a magician with magical substances and mantras appear to be actual horses, oxen, women, and so on; but, in fact, these illusions are not real horses and such. Similarly, objects that appear during the post-meditation period should be thought of as resembling illusions. In short, during the post-meditation period all our perceptions should be sustained by the understanding of the lack of true existence that we gained while absorbed in meditation on emptiness.

· 3 ·

BRINGING UNFAVORABLE CONDITIONS

into the

PATH TO ENLIGHTENMENT

---

*When the vessel and its contents are filled with
negativities,
Transform these unfavorable conditions into the path
to enlightenment.*

Conditions in the worldly realms (the vessel) are such
that the environmental results of the ten non-virtues are
very abundant, with many tree stumps, thorns, bits of
brick, ravines, stones, and so forth. Likewise, conditions
are such that sentient beings' (the contents) thoughts
are none other than afflictions, their deeds are none
other than negative actions, and so forth. Due to these
conditions, the gods and *nagas* (serpent-like creatures
who may possess supernormal powers) who delight in
goodness are losing strength, while the demons, hinderers, beings of perverse prayers,[4] and elemental spirits who delight in evil are gaining strength. As a result,
all Dharma practitioners experience great harm.

During this period in which we are entangled in
unfavorable conditions, reflect that adverse conditions
are favorable conditions; interferences are assistants;
and harmful beings, spirits, hinderers, and elemental

spirits are virtuous friends. Doing so, we will transform unfavorable conditions into a method to achieve enlightenment.

Becoming a Child of the Buddhas As a result of transgressing the morality of the ten virtuous actions in the past, we experience various unpleasant environmental conditions. For example, our place of rebirth may have many thorns, rough ground, rubbish, deep ravines, and so forth. In fact, whatever faults there are in our environment, they are the results of the negative actions we committed in the past. Due to our previous non-virtuous actions, we will also experience internal, or personal, unpleasant conditions, such as having to live with people whose thoughts are afflictions and whose actions are non-virtuous. In addition, when we allow our morality to degenerate, the gods and other beings on the side of virtue—who themselves are Dharma practitioners—become unhappy and cease to help us. Instead, the spirits and other beings on the side of non-virtue become more powerful and attempt to control and harm us. Likewise, human beings harm us, and we experience illness and many difficulties. When such experiences happen, it is necessary as practitioners of mind training to transform them into positive conditions, for this will enable us to gain spiritual realizations. We can do so by, for example, seeing harmful beings as virtuous friends who help us generate the mind of enlightenment. By practicing like this, we will be able to transform all adverse conditions into a method for developing the precious mind of enlightenment.

Immediately apply whatever you meet to meditation.

In any circumstance whatsoever (monastery or town, human or non-human companions, contentment or suffering, good or bad, sudden illness, spirits, enemies, and so forth) and no matter what terrible suffering occurs, make requests to the guru and the [Three] Jewels and practice whatever mind training you can.

During our lifetime, we might live in a city, a small village, or even a monastery. We will meet many kinds of people, both good and bad, and perhaps even non-human spirits. At times we will experience a good life, while at others we will find ourselves in difficult situations, such as becoming seriously ill or being

harmed by spirits. We will also experience various feelings, sometimes happiness, and other times suffering. In all of these situations, we should remember the guru and the Three Jewels and
pray to them. Then, we should immediately apply whatever
problem we are experiencing to meditation so that it can con-
tribute to our development of the mind of enlightenment.

*Bringing
Unfavorable
Conditions
into the
Path of
Enlightenment*

Possess the four preparations, the supreme method.

1. The first preparation is as follows. Whenever suffering occurs and you develop the wish to be free from
   it, put effort into virtuous practices of body, speech,
   and mind, such as making offerings to the [Three]
   Jewels, rendering service to the Sangha, giving *tormas* (ritual offering cakes) to elemental spirits, and so
   forth. After doing so, request blessings to be sick if it
   is better to be sick, to be cured if it is better to be
   cured, and to die if it is better to die. Be sure to make
   these requests while stilling hope and fear.

2. The second preparation is to confess your negativities by way of remedial prayers and the four [oppo-
   nent] forces:
   a. The force of total repudiation is to regret nega-
      tivities committed in the past.
   b. The force of turning away from faults in the
      future is to decide not to commit [negativities]
      from now on, even at the risk of one's life.
   c. The force of the basis is to go for refuge and gen-
      erate the mind [of enlightenment].
   d. The force of applying antidotes is to meditate on
      emptiness, recite *mantra-dharanis* (sacred syllables
      holding the essence of Dharma), and so forth.
Confess your negativities by way of these four.

3. The third preparation, that of making offerings to
   spirits, is as follows. Give spirit-tormas to harmful
   beings, spirits, hinderers, and elemental spirits while
   saying, "Because you help me train my mind you are
   very kind. Please once again give me the unwanted
   sufferings of all sentient beings, my former mothers."

4. The fourth preparation, that of offering tormas to
   the Dharma protectors, is to give offering tormas in

accordance with the procedure of the holy beings of the past. Having given [the Dharma protectors] "a hundred tormas," *tsa-sur,*[5] and so on, make them pacify conditions adverse to Dharma and create concordant conditions. Entrust them to perform the enlightened activities that would allow you to transform unfavorable conditions into the path to enlightenment.

The four preparations are:

1. *Striving in virtuous practices when suffering occurs.* When suffering occurs, we tend to wish to be free from it. This desire is itself an interference to the practice of mind training. As practitioners of mind training, we should not wish to be free even from situations of great suffering. Instead we should transform all our physical, verbal, and mental actions into virtue, for example, by requesting the Three Jewels to grant us blessings to be able to experience whatever is of most benefit to our Dharma practice, such as to be sick if it is better to be sick, to be cured if it is better to be cured, and to die if it is better to die. We can also engage in virtuous practices by rendering service to a spiritual community, such as a monastery or Dharma center, and by giving torma offerings to the elemental spirits who belong to the hungry ghost realm. Whichever of these practices we choose to do, we should do it free of hope and fear. In other words, we should not be overly optimistic that we will completely recover from a serious illness, nor should we be overly pessimistic by thinking that it will definitely worsen.

2. *Confessing negativities by applying the four opponent forces.* Our negative actions are of varying degrees, some being heavier, or more serious, and others being lighter, or less serious. Light negativities include actions such as accidentally killing an insect, stealing a tiny worthless object, or telling a very small lie. On the other hand, the heaviest of negative actions are those created by the mind — covetousness, malice, and wrong view — because it is the mind that initially motivates us to engage in any action. Among these three negative mental actions, most of us probably do not have wrong views very often. Covetousness and malice, on the other hand, are more common, and cause us to commit grave negative actions.

Malice—the wish to harm those whom we do not like—tends to arise more often than covetousness. In some people malice is very obvious, while in others it tends to be more hidden. Even in a particular person, malice may vary: sometimes it may be very weak, while at others times it may be very strong. Because malice harms us much more than the people toward whom we develop it, it would be much wiser to abandon malice rather than nourishing and mentally holding on to it.

Another disadvantage of malice is that it destroys even the virtues created in past lives; all the energy and time we put into creating virtuous actions thus goes to waste. In fact, the reason that we should always dedicate our merits for the attainment of enlightenment is to ensure that they will not be destroyed in the future by negative thoughts such as malice.

In addition to confessing whatever negative actions we have committed in this life, we need to purify the many negative actions, such as the five actions of immediate retribution, that we committed in previous lives.

The four opponent forces are:

a. The force of total repudiation. Understanding that if we do not confess our negative actions we will definitely be reborn in the lower realms, we develop a sense of regret for having committed such actions. This regret, called the force of total repudiation, should be similar to the regret of someone who knows that he has mistakenly ingested poisoned food.

The force of repudiation can be compared to digging a trench to allow water to flow around a tree so that naturally its roots will weaken and it will fall down. In other words, if we intensely regret having committed negative actions we will naturally wish to engage in remedial Dharma practice, such as doing prostrations, making offerings, and reciting prayers. We become like a person who, having eaten poisoned food, is very worried about dying and urgently seeks a solution to be free from this danger.

b. The force of turning away from faults in the future. As a result of negative actions we did not have an opportunity to meet a guru in the past who could have taught us how to confess our negativities. Hence, we created many negative actions out of ignorance. But now that we know how to confess our negativities, we should make a strong determination, or resolution, to not commit them ever again, even at the cost of our lives. This is the force of turning away from faults in the future. We may know, however, that we are unable to truthfully vow to never repeat a specific negative action again: we might even know that we are likely to repeat the action as soon as tomorrow. In such cases, Kyabje Trijang Dorje Chang, the junior tutor of His Holiness the XIV Dalai Lama, advised us to resolve to, at the very least, not commit that action again today.

c. The force of the basis. The force of the basis is comprised of going for refuge to the Three Jewels and generating the mind of enlightenment toward all sentient beings. This force is called *the basis* because going for refuge and generating the mind of enlightenment purify respectively the negative actions we committed in regard to the Three Jewels and other sentient beings, the bases.

When we go for refuge and generate the mind of enlightenment, it is not enough to merely repeat the words of a particular prayer; rather, we should do so from the depths of our hearts. In this way, these practices will be much more meaningful to us.

d. The force of applying antidotes. The force of applying antidotes consists of performing prostrations, making offerings, reciting mantras and prayers, meditating on emptiness, and so forth. Engaging in these actions is the *application of antidotes* because they are the actual antidotes that we apply to purify our negative actions. While the force of total repudiation is compared to causing water to flow around the base of a tree to make it fall down — an action that in itself does not have much power — the force of applying antidotes is compared to using an ax to directly cut down a tree. In other words, when we apply this force, we engage in a practice that directly purifies our negative actions.

Although it is essential to have all four forces present when confessing negativities, the two most important ones are the force of total repudiation and the force of turning way from faults in the future. When such regret and determination are present, we automatically confess our negative actions.

In short, by appreciating the benefits of these four forces we will naturally find the energy to apply them. In the end, the efficacy of our purification practice depends very much on the mind. Not only is it the mind that motivates us to do negative actions, but it is also the mind that confesses and purifies them. I put so much emphasis on the practice of confession because people sometimes are a bit careless about this practice, but that carelessness is a great mistake. For beginners, it is extremely important to do confession because only after having confessed and purified negative actions can higher levels of realization be achieved.

3. *Making offerings to spirits.* Instead of seeking revenge, when evil spirits harm us, we should offer them tormas and so forth as a sign of our gratitude. While engaged in such practices, we should think, "Thank you for all the harm you have given me, thereby helping me to develop the mind of enlightenment. Please continue to cause me even more problems and suffering in the future so that I will have more occasions to train my mind."

*Bringing
Unfavorable
Conditions
into the
Path of
Enlightenment*

4. *Offering tormas to the Dharma protectors.* In the past, holy beings made offerings to their own specific Dharma protectors so as to receive help from them in their Dharma practice. Likewise, we must entrust the Dharma protectors to help us train in the mind of enlightenment by offering tormas and making other offerings. While making such offerings, we should request their aid, saying, "Dharma protectors, help me to be able to transform all adverse conditions into the path to enlightenment, and bestow on me perfect conditions for my Dharma practice."

Some people, apart from engaging in the mind training practices, also perform rituals and recite prayers to avoid experiencing problems, such as an illness. But when we are authentically practicing mind training, we should voluntarily take upon ourselves any suffering that occurs. We should think, "In the past while practicing 'taking and giving' I made prayers to be able to take other beings' sufferings upon myself and give my happiness to them. Now I am experiencing that very suffering." Thinking in this way, we should rejoice that our prayers have been realized. In addition, we can gladly make use of this opportunity by thinking, "Through my experiencing this illness may all other sentient beings be free from it."

When we practice mind training it is not enough to merely know the words of a particular text. Instead, it is essential to deeply understand the meaning of the text and to meditate on it again and again. In this way, we will develop our mind training practice into a strong and stable foundation on which to gain higher realizations. In fact, mind training is like the first step in our Dharma practice; having gained skill in it, we can then progress to higher practices. To reach the top rung of a ladder, we begin by climbing up the first rung and then continue on until we safely reach the top; similarly, we will reach the completion of our Dharma practice only by successfully accomplishing each step, one at a time.

· 4 ·

INTEGRATING THE PRACTICES

in a

SINGLE LIFETIME

In brief, the essence of the instructions
is to apply the five forces.

In brief, the essence of the instructions is the practice of the [following] five forces:

1. *The force of resolution.* Make a strong determination, thinking, "From now until I attain buddhahood (or until I die), in this year and this month destroying the burgeoning afflictions, I will never allow my body, speech, and mind to be separated from the instructions for training in the mind of enlightenment."

2. *The force of familiarity.* Continually and repeatedly put effort into familiarizing and acquainting yourself with the mind that would quickly generate the precious mind [of enlightenment].

3. *The force of the white seed.* Strive to complete the two collections. They are: (1) the collection of merit, which arises from generosity, morality, and meditation and is the cause for the generation of the precious mind of enlightenment that has not yet been generated, for the abiding of one that has already been generated, and for the

increasing of one that is abiding; and (2) the collection of exalted wisdom, which is meditation on meditative stabilization and emptiness.

4. *The power of rejection.* Through seeing the disadvantages of cherishing yourself and neglecting others, continually strive to reject and eliminate self-grasping by way of its antidote.

5. *The force of prayer.* Make fervent dedications and prayers, thinking, "May the precious mind of enlightenment increase in dependence on the strength of the roots of virtue of the three times that I have gathered with my three doors."

The five [forces], the practice of all the Dharma of the Great Vehicle, are said to be encompassed by a single HUM.

The essence of mind training is the practice of the five forces:

1. The force of resolution is to make a strong determination to never allow yourself to be separated from the instructions on mind training; in other words, never allow yourself to be separated from the mind of enlightenment. To this end, we must firmly decide, "From now until I attain enlightenment, or at least until I die, I will destroy all the various kinds of afflictions this very year and this very month." Although in general the term *affliction* refers to the mental obscurations that obstruct liberation, in this context it specifically refers to the mind that cherishes oneself and neglects others. Therefore, destroying the afflictions refers to gaining some control, or power, over the self-cherishing attitude. Just as a fire can be successfully extinguished when forcefully countered, likewise, when we become aware of the self-cherishing mind, we should attempt immediately to forcefully counter and put a stop to it.

To train ourselves in cherishing others, we should mentally take upon ourselves all the sufferings that have yet to ripen on other sentient beings. For example, while we are performing physical activities, such as prostrations, making offerings, or working for a Dharma purpose, we should think that by doing so we are creating the cause for all the sufferings of other sentient beings to ripen upon ourselves. We can also think like this when we do verbal activities, such as reciting prayers and mantras, and when we engage in mental activities, such as meditating on the mind of enlightenment and emptiness. We should imagine that as a result of this practice, other sentient beings become free from all their problems.

By keeping the attitude of cherishing others constantly present in our minds, we will continually develop the mind of enlightenment. The generation of such positive thoughts is the real practice of mind training.

2. The force of familiarity is to repeatedly familiarize and acquaint ourselves with the mind of enlightenment until it arises continuously and spontaneously. To do this, we need to concentrate initially on becoming very familiar with the mind training practices. Practicing in this way, they will gradually become easier and easier until one day we will generate the actual mind of enlightenment.

3. The force of the white seed is to generate the mind of enlightenment that has not yet been generated, stabilize that which has been generated, and increase that which has become stable. For this purpose, we need to engage in the practice of the six perfections: generosity, morality, patience, effort, concentration, and wisdom. The first five perfections are included in the collection of merit, while the last, the perfection of wisdom, is included in the collection of wisdom. With the support of these two collections, we will be able to increase the strength of the mind of enlightenment.

If we wish to engage in the practice of generosity, we must initially develop the mental attitude that wishes to give. On this basis, we should begin to give away our possessions to others. However, because it is not always easy in the beginning to give away our belongings, we can start by first training in a gradual way. For example, someone who is extremely tightfisted can begin the practice with something as simple as holding a small object in the right hand and passing it to the left hand and then passing it back again while thinking, "Now I am giving this object to my left hand. Now I am giving it to my right."

In a certain sutra, there is a story that illustrates how miserly people can be. This story concerns a foe destroyer whose mother was quite rich but very stingy. Even though she was wealthy, she did not eat properly nor did she enjoy her many possessions. Moreover, she was unable to give away even the tiniest thing. The

45

foe destroyer knew that if his mother did not change her behavior, she would be reborn in the hungry ghost realm, so he advised her to make offerings to the Three Jewels. In spite of her son's sage advice, the miserly woman remained reluctant to give away anything at all. After many unsuccessful admonishments, the foe destroyer finally gave her a piece of the yellow cloth used for making one of the robes worn by fully ordained monks. He then accompanied her to offer it to Shakyamuni Buddha. Although she did manage to offer the cloth to Buddha, she stole it back the same evening! The next day her son once again made her offer it to the Buddha, but that evening she again stole it back! In desperation, after convincing his mother to offer the cloth once more, the foe destroyer finally cut up the piece of cloth and sewed the bits and pieces onto the cushions that belonged to the monastic community. This time his mother did not take the cloth back —it was no longer any use to her!

Reflecting on this story and other examples of miserliness, we should try to be more generous and less tightfisted. People who possess plenty of material things can use whatever they need for themselves, but, at the very least, they should offer whatever they do not use to the Three Jewels or give it to the poor. If they do not do this, they will create the cause to take rebirth in the hungry ghost realm.

While practicing generosity and the other perfections, we should always remember how very fortunate we are to have this opportunity. In fact, we have all the tools—the methods, knowledge, material objects, and so forth—that are needed to accumulate merit and wisdom.

4. The force of rejection is to reject selfish thoughts— thoughts that make us look down on and neglect others while cherishing ourselves. We should apply the antidotes to this self-cherishing mind by meditating on the disadvantages of cherishing ourselves and the advantages of cherishing others. Recall that the self-cherishing attitude causes us much suffering and many problems, while the mind that cherishes others brings us great benefit and happiness. Having understood this, we should work to gradually abandon the mind of self-cherishing.

5. The force of prayer is to dedicate all the virtues of body, speech, and mind that we created in the past, those that we are creating in the present, and those that we will create in the future

to the development of the mind of enlightenment for the sake of all sentient beings. We create virtue with our bodies by doing prostrations, circumambulating monasteries and stupas, and other such activites. With our speech we accumulate virtue by reciting mantras, prayers, and so forth. And with our minds we create virtue by engaging in practices such as meditating on emptiness.

The five forces are a synthesis of all the Great Vehicle instructions, and through practicing them all Dharma practices can be integrated in a single lifetime. It is said that the practice of the five forces is encompassed by a single HUM.

The Great Vehicle instructions on transference are those very five forces.

1. *The instruction of the white seed.* Sell whatever belongings you have without clinging and then liberally make offerings to whatever is of greatest merit, the [Three] Jewels, and so forth.

2. *The instruction of prayer.* Offer the seven-limb [prayer] to the guru and the [Three] Jewels and then fervently pray, "May I, in the intermediate state and in all my lives, never be separated from the two kinds of precious mind [of enlightenment]. Please especially bless me to meet a guru who will reveal this Dharma to me."

3. *The instruction of rejection.* Abandon and eradicate cherishing even your body and life because as a result of not having abandoned clinging to your body, possessions, friends, relatives, and so forth and instead cherishing them, you have been made to suffer in the past and are still being made to suffer.

4. *The instruction of resolution.* Develop a strong aspiration, thinking, "I will train in the precious mind of enlightenment even in the intermediate state."

5. *The instruction of familiarity.* At the time of death, lie in the lion position on your right side and block your right nostril with the ring finger of your right hand. As you inhale and exhale, fervently practice taking and giving. In addition, cease the grasping at true existence by reflecting that cyclic existence and nirvana, birth and death, and so forth are none other than mere

appearances to a mistaken mind and do not exist inherently. You should be able to die while alternately meditating on these two kinds of precious mind [of enlightenment].

The five instructions of the Great Vehicle on the transference of consciousness should be practiced when we are certain that we are definitely about to die.

1. *The instruction of the white seed.* As we near death, it is important to diminish our tendency to grasp at our belongings by giving them away without clinging to them. They can be given to superior recipients, such as the Three Jewels, or to inferior ones, such as the poor and the needy. If we do not do this, our attachment to our possessions will prevent us from making progress on the spiritual path, just as a chain bound around our ankles prevents us from moving.

Furthermore, when we are actually dying, it is best not to worry at this point about making a will because this could aggravate grasping and attachment to our possessions. Because the best way to die is calmly, with as little talking as possible, it is best to make a will while we are still healthy and free of mental and physical problems. In addition, a dying person should not be preoccupied with eating, nor should his or her friends and relatives encourage him or her to eat. But most important, a dying person should be free from sadness, regret, and discouragement, such as thinking that he or she did not accomplish anything worthwhile during his or her life. In this way, one will be able to die peacefully and without excessive worry about where one will be reborn.

It is said that we receive our Dharma practice "grades" at the time of death, when the subtle mind is about to leave the physical body. Only at this time do find out how well we have actually practiced in that excellent practitioners experience death joyfully, as though returning home with a happy mind; average practitioners experience death free of regret and worry; those who have practiced very little experience a great reluctance to die, as well as fear and anxiety.

2. *The instruction of prayer.* When we are very close to death, weak and no longer able to move, it is very important to offer

48

prayers, such as the seven-limb prayer, to the Three Jewels. We should also make specific prayers in which we pray that in the intermediate rebirth and all our future lives we never be separated from the two precious minds of enlightenment and always have the good fortune to meet gurus who teach the holy Dharma.

3. *The instruction of rejection.* A dying person generally finds him- or herself surrounded by sad and weeping friends and relatives, thus causing attachment to arise in his or her mind. However, it is very important when we are close to death to not be attached to our friends, parents, relatives, and even to our own bodies. To diminish this attachment, we should think, "As a result of attachment to friends, relatives, and others in my past lives, I have been reborn again and again in cyclic existence and in all these rebirths, I have had to continually experience various kinds of suffering. If I am once again unable to abandon such attachment, it will only bring me further rebirths and more suffering in cyclic existence." By thinking in this way, we will be able to completely cut off attachment at the time of death.

To help diminish attachment, it is also advisable that a dying person not look around too much at the surrounding people. Rather, it is best to keep one's eyes closed and remain in a peaceful mental state by meditating on the mind of enlightenment and making prayers to the Three Jewels.

4. *The instruction of resolution.* At the time of death, when the mind is about to depart from the body, we should make a strong resolution to never give up the mind training practices and to train ourselves in the mind of enlightenment even in the intermediate state.

5. *The instruction of familiarity.* At the moment of death, we should lie, as did Shakyamuni Buddha, in the lion position: lying on the right side, the palm of the right hand under the right cheek, both legs almost fully extended, and the left arm resting on the left side of the body. Then we should alternately meditate on the two kinds of mind of enlightenment. We do so at times by practicing taking and giving and at other times by eliminating the grasping at true existence through contemplating the fact that death and rebirth are like illusions.

At the time of death it is generally taught that one should block the right nostril with the right ring finger to stop the flow of non-virtuous winds, or energies. However, practitioners of mind training, who are combining the practice of taking and giving with the inhalation and exhalation of the breath, can omit blocking the right nostril.

Cherish this behavior.

> With respect to your behavior at the point of death, it is extremely important that you not be separated from the five forces, the Great Vehicle instructions on the transference [of consciousness]. Therefore, you should be certain to carefully exert yourself in [practicing] them. Since the signs of a continuous Dharma practice and our skill in practicing it will become evident at this time, we should develop the ability to die in a state of contentment thinking, "Even if I have to remain in the dark hole of the hell of Unrelenting Torment for the welfare of all sentient beings, my former mothers, I will gladly experience it."

In this context, behavior refers to the mind training practices that are to be especially cherished at the time of death. At the time of death we discover how much skill in the mind of enlightenment we have gained through our lifetime practice of the five forces. If we have practiced mind training, when we are about to die, we will neither be worried nor make such prayers as, "May I never be reborn in hell and may I always experience happiness." Instead, we will be able to pray, "May I be reborn in hell for the sake of all my former mother sentient beings who are tormented there."

The five forces, the Great Vehicle instructions on the transference of consciousness, should not be taken lightly. Instead, we should take these instructions seriously and put the five forces into practice in our day-to-day life as much as possible.

·5·

THE   MEASURE

of a

TRAINED   MIND

Combine all the Dharma into one intention.

Since all the Dharma of the Great and Lesser Vehicles
was taught solely as an antidote to self-grasping, the
measure of our Dharma practice is the extent to which
it acts as an antidote to self-grasping. This is also the
scale that weighs Dharma practitioners.

Anything that acts as an antidote to self-grasping is Dharma practice. On the other hand, even though we may engage in a great
variety of practices that may appear to be spiritual, if they do not
act to destroy our self-grasping, they are not Dharma practice.
Therefore, this is also said to be the weighing scales that deter-
mines who is a real Dharma practitioner.

Of the two witnesses, rely on the primary one.

Even though others' undisturbed minds might be suit-
able as witnesses, since it is possible to please ordinary
worldly beings with a mere bit of good external behavior,
do not take them as your primary [witness]. However,
the [Three] Jewels clearly and unimpededly see us during

the three times, day and night; therefore, there is nothing whatsoever that they and the guru do not know. For this reason, always abandon hypocrisy.

Your own mind is not hidden from you, so it is the primary [witness]. Since you cannot deceive yourself, you cannot fool yourself, and you cannot shame yourself, you are your own primary witness. This is also a measure of your mind training.

The first witness is other people, while the second is our own minds. Other people are our witnesses because, when we commit negative actions, they criticize us, while when we behave well, they praise and respect us. However, although our physical and verbal actions may appear to be quite good, our minds, the primary witness, might be overwhelmed by the three mental poisons—attachment, hatred, and ignorance. If our minds are filled with these poisons, yet we are unaware of it, then we will be merely deceiving ourselves, no matter how good we might appear to be. This is self-deception because when we commit actions contrary to the Dharma, we completely destroy our own future happiness, even though we may fulfill our wishes in this life. On the other hand, if we know that we are engaging in non-virtuous actions yet do not control our minds, we deceive and displease the Three Jewels who perceive our minds and our every action. For this reason, the Three Jewels and our guru, who embodies the Three Jewels, can also be considered a primary witness.

We should take care not to deceive our external witnesses, other people, by pretending to practice Dharma, and we should be equally concerned not to cheat our inner witnesses, our own mind and our gurus. In brief, when we train in the mind of enlightenment it is essential to avoid hypocrisy, such as acting in one way while thinking in another; instead, we should always act sincerely. This, in fact, is a measure that accurately indicates how much progress we have made with respect to training in the mind of enlightenment.

Always rely on mental happiness alone.

Whenever others falsely criticize you even though you have not done anything, whenever you experience physical and mental illnesses and pain, in short, whenever any undesired suffering occurs, delight in it and think, "I can bring [this experience] into the path of mind training without allowing my [practice] to deteriorate." In this way, make your mind stable. When this [attitude] is present, your mind is trained.

At times other people may scold, curse, blame, belittle, or accuse us, even though we have not done anything wrong. On another occasion we may become temporarily sick or even contract a serious life-threatening illness. However, if we are sincerely training our minds, we should not let these experiences make us unhappy. Instead, we should remain happy by accepting the suffering and looking on it as an excellent opportunity to train the mind. This ability to voluntarily accept and endure suffering is another measure that indicates how much we have trained our minds.

The measure of being trained is to no longer regress.

Beginning with the preliminary Dharma [practices] — such as [the meditations on] the great meaning of the freedoms and endowments and the difficulty of obtaining them — you should proceed up to the training in the ultimate mind [of enlightenment]. The measure of being trained [in each of these] is to no longer regress. For example, when you no longer squander your freedoms and endowments no matter what the circumstances, and when you generate in your continua the genuine mind that is able to take their essence, then your mind is trained [in that practice].

Initially, we should train our minds by meditating on the great meaning of this precious human rebirth, death-impermanence, and so forth. In other words, we should first train in the stages of the path of practitioners of inferior scope and subsequently in those of practitioners of middling scope. Only after these two scopes have been completed should we begin to train in the mind of enlightenment. By developing our practice gradually in this way, we will make steady progress in mind training without regression.

To be trained is to possess the five signs of greatness.

Do not be separated from these five [signs]:

1. The [sign of] a great bodhisattva is that, having seen

that it is the essence of all the scriptures, you train at all times in the precious mind of enlightenment of the Great Vehicle.

2. The [sign of] a great holder of discipline is that, having gained conviction in the law of action and result, you shrink away from [committing] even the slightest fault.

3. The [sign of] a great ascetic is that you endure hardships in order to destroy the afflictions in your continuum.

4. The [sign of] a great trainee in virtue is that the activities of your body and speech are never separated from the ten Dharma activities of the Great Vehicle.[6]

5. The [sign of] a great yogi is that you continually cultivate the yogas that prevent the degeneration of the precious mind of enlightenment and its auxiliary branches.[7]

1. The first sign of having trained the mind is to become a great bodhisattva who, having come to the understanding that the essence of all the Great Vehicle teachings is the mind of enlightenment, constantly trains in and develops it.

2. The second sign of having trained the mind is to become a great holder of discipline who, having belief in and respect for the law of action and result, avoids even the slightest of negative actions, such as killing an ant or making a rude gesture, knowing that in the future such actions will bring the result of suffering.

3. The third sign of having trained the mind is to become a great ascetic who is able to bear any hardships for the purpose of destroying the afflictions.

4. The fourth sign of having trained the mind is to become a great trainee in virtue who is never separated from the ten Dharma activities, the practices of the Great Vehicle, no matter what physical or verbal activities one is engaged in.

5. The fifth sign of having trained the mind is to become a great yogi who constantly cultivates the precious mind of enlightenment through training in the causes for generating it, such as the meditation on the sevenfold causes and effect.[8]

You are trained when able even if distracted.

An expert horseman never falls from a horse even
though he is distracted. Likewise, a measure [that indi-
cates] you have [successfully] trained your mind is to be
able to transform [unpleasant experiences] into an aid
to mind training without becoming angry. For example, when someone speaks to you in an undesirable
fashion, addressing you contemptuously, verbally abus-
ing you, swearing at you, deriding you, or falsely accus-
ing you, you [respond by] thinking, "Even Buddha
himself had many such [experiences]. Since I have not
yet abandoned malice, this is the result of my own negative actions."

A person who has genuinely trained his or her mind is compared
to an experienced horseman who, even though distracted, would
not fall from a galloping or untamed horse. Similarly, a person
who is well trained in the mind of enlightenment is capable of
tolerating problems caused by other people and transforms such
seemingly adverse conditions into a method for developing the
mind of enlightenment. For example, criticized or wrongly
blamed, a practitioner of mind training does not become angry;
instead he or she reflects, "Even Buddha, an omniscient being,
was criticized and disparaged by other people, including his
cousin Devadatta. Yet compared to the Buddha, I am a very ordinary and insignificant person. The only reason that in this life
there are many people who harm, criticize, and accuse me is that
I did not abandon malice in the past."

In short, the ability to bear difficulties and transform them
into a method to increase the mind of enlightenment is a measure that indicates how well we have trained our minds.

· 6 ·

THE COMMITMENTS
of
MIND TRAINING

Constantly train in the three general points.

1. Do not transgress the commitments of mind training. In other words, do not ignore even the slightest training.

2. Do not be reckless. Do not engage in such reckless behavior as digging in hazardous⁹ earth, cutting down hazardous trees, churning up hazardous water, going to places where there are contagious diseases rather than avoiding them, and so forth.

3. Do not be partial. Abandon the three partialities:
   a. tolerating harm from humans while not tolerating harm from gods and spirits,
   b. being patient with one's superiors while disparaging one's inferiors,
   c. being affectionate toward one's friends while hating one's enemies.

The first commitment of mind training is to keep all eighteen commitments of mind training very carefully without transgressing even the slightest one. In addition, because people who are training in the mind of enlightenment have in general taken the bodhisattva vows, this first commitment also includes not transgressing the eighteen root and forty-six secondary bodhisattva vows.

The second commitment of mind training is to not be reckless and arrogant, for example, by thinking that due to our realizations we can do whatever we like, such as digging in the earth where nagas live, cutting down trees inhabited by spirits, and being careless when visiting people with contagious diseases. When we are practicing mind training, we should never arrogantly show other people that we have attained realizations or that we have generated the mind of enlightenment.

The third commitment of mind training is to avoid being partial, or biased, toward others. We might be able to endure harm caused by human beings, but find it difficult to tolerate that caused by evil spirits; as a result, we might perform various rituals to destroy them. Or we might be able to endure being humiliated by a powerful or wealthy person, but not be able to tolerate being despised or belittled by a person whom we consider in some manner to be our inferior. Or we might be willing to help people who are our friends, but not those whom we identify as enemies. But as practitioners of mind training, we should be impartial toward all people at all times.

4. *Change your attitude, but remain natural.*

Having changed your mental attitude, act in accordance with the mind training of the Great Vehicle without artificiality. Unperceived by others, inconspicuously and effectively mature your continuum. The fourth commitment of mind training is to change our attitude without revealing our spiritual practice to other people. In other words, we may be practicing perfectly and have achieved very good results; nevertheless, it is better to hide our progress and to show others that we are just practicing a little and have achieved only a small result.

5. *Do not mention [others'] impaired limbs.*

Even if others have defects, such as a handicap, blindness, deafness, dumbness, imperfect limbs, or corrupt morality, never mention them. Also do not even criticize, for example, non-humans by calling them such names as "evil spirits." As it says in *Rays of Sunlight Mind Training*, "Abandon wrathful subjugation. Practice forcefully." Pacify violence with love and compassion toward, for example, beings who are not human. Exhorting them not to harm others plants the seed of liberation even in the continua of harmful beings, and is the cause of both your own and others' happiness. On the other hand, you might perform wrathful fire pujas, wrathful torma offerings,[10] wrathful suppression of evil spirits, and so forth through wrathful tantric practices. But due to performing these practices, in the short term many different illnesses will afflict everyone, both yourself and others, and any activities you do will not become a [spiritual] path. In the long term, as a result of the resentment of these non-humans, such [wrathful activities] will cause us harm in both this and future lives.

Likewise, with regard to human beings as well, when you speak gently, have good intentions, and do whatever benefits them, whatever you do in this life will become a [spiritual] path, and [your behavior] will become an object of everyone's praise. This [way of behaving] will thus become a cause of happiness in both this and future lives.

On the contrary, you might harm others, whether through direct or indirect means, such as malicious speech, harsh words, evil intentions, and deception. But if you do so, in the short term whatever activities you do will not become a [spiritual] path. And as a result of being considered everyone's enemy, [your behavior] will become none other than a source of harm for yourself, both in the short and long term. Therefore, you should never wrathfully subdue anyone, whether human or non-human, out of anger. Instead, you should persist undistractedly at all times and in all situations in the wrathful subjugation of your own obstinate continuum.

The fifth commitment of mind training is to not speak of other people's shortcomings, such as telling them that they lack such-and-such a quality or pointing out their impaired limbs. In addition, we should not insult others by calling them disparaging names and so forth, such as offending non-human spirits by calling them evil. If we insult them, apart from it interfering with the success of our mind training practices, we would also run the risk of these spirits deciding to wreak havoc on us by causing us all kinds of problems. If this were to happen, we might, in turn, think to stop them by employing some type of wrathful practice to destroy them, such as reciting wrathful mantras or making torma offerings. However, because such beings are clairvoyant, they would know who is harming them; hence, they would hold a grudge while seeking an opportunity to avenge themselves. Therefore, it would be much better if, right from the outset, we were to develop loving kindness toward these spirits who, knowing our positive thoughts, would consequently turn to helping us.

We also should try to benefit human beings as much as possible because the long-term outcome of such behavior is always much more beneficial. In contrast, if we were to use our authority or speak harshly to get what we want, we might enjoy some short-term success, but in the future, that person would likely harm us out of resentment.

In short, we should employ forceful means to destroy not other sentient beings, but our own mental afflictions, in particular the self-cherishing mind. As Shantideva clearly states in his text *Engaging in the Bodhisattva Deeds,* "When ordinary enemies are banished from one place, they retreat and settle in another country. Then, having restored their power, they return [to fight again]. The afflictions, however, are not that kind of enemy."

6. Do not think about others' affairs.

> Whenever we see faults in sentient beings in general, and in Dharma practitioners in particular, we should abandon the attitude that conceives of such faults by thinking, "This is a result of my own impure appearances. How else could they have such faults?"

The sixth commitment of mind training is to abandon looking for and judging other sentient beings' faults, including those of other Dharma practitioners. Instead, we should train our minds in pure appearance by thinking that when we see such-and-such a defect in someone, it is because we project such imagined faults on other people due to our own impure appearances. By practicing in this way, we will be able to protect ourselves from the tendency to judge others.

7. Initially, purify whatever affliction is the strongest.

Check which affliction in your continuum is the strongest. Then, having amassed all the Dharma as an antidote to it, initially abandon that very one. As the *Rays of Sunlight Mind Training* says, "Initially, purify whichever one is the most gross."

The seventh commitment of mind training is to initially purify whatever affliction is strongest in our continua. To do so, we must begin by examining the many kinds of afflictions that arise in our minds. Then, once we have identified the strongest one, we should apply the specific antidote to this particular affliction before going on to eliminate other less troubling afflictions.

8. Give up all hope of reward.

Do not think to merely attain liberation for the sake of your own desired happiness; instead, strive to attain liberation for the welfare of all sentient beings, your former mothers.

The eighth commitment of mind training is to abandon hope and expectation of receiving some personal benefit from our mind training practice, such as the attainment of merely our own liberation from cyclic existence. Instead, we should put effort into achieving the state of perfect complete enlightenment for the sake of other sentient beings by constantly reminding ourselves that we are practicing mind training to help them achieve happiness.

9. Avoid poisoned food.

If it is mixed with the mind that grasps at true existence or self-cherishing, any virtue you create will actually be fatal to your liberation, just as food mixed with poison is fatal. Therefore, do not mix your roots of virtue with grasping at true existence and self-cherishing.

The ninth commitment of mind training is to not mix virtue with the minds of self-grasping and self-cherishing. When virtuous actions are done in conjunction with these mental states, those actions will actually end up harming us by cutting our virtues and preventing liberation, just as food mixed with poison endangers our life. Therefore, when we practice, for example, generosity toward the poor or toward the Three Jewels, we should be extremely careful not to mix this positive action with either the thought that phenomena are truly existent or the thought that oneself is more important than others. Instead, we should strive to completely abandon these two mental states.

10. Do not hold a grudge.

> Having developed a grudge against someone who has harmed you, abandon never letting go of that resentful state of mind.

The tenth commitment of mind training is to abandon holding a grudge against those who have harmed us, for example, by physically striking or verbally insulting us. We should always avoid developing resentment and never plan to retaliate at some time in the future.

11. Do not respond to malicious talk.

> Even though others may say negative words that seem to almost split your heart, strive to not say a single word of harm in response.

The eleventh commitment of mind training is to not retaliate with harmful words even when other people wound us deeply by mocking, scolding, or speaking harshly to us.

12. Do not lie in ambush.

> Do not behave in such a way that, deeply resenting the harm done to you by another, when one day a chance to avenge yourself finally arises, you retaliate.

According to the twelfth commitment of mind training, if you have been harmed by someone and did not immediately have the opportunity to retaliate, you should not wait, as though lying in ambush, for an opportunity to return that harm.

13. Do not strike to the core.

> Do not spy out other people's faults, do not recite life-mantras that cause harm to non-humans, and so forth.

The thirteenth commitment of mind training is, although we know someone's faults and weaknesses, to not reveal them to others with the intention of harming that person.

14. Do not put the load of a dzo[11] *on an ox.*

Do not divert to others, with various deceitful means, the badly performed responsibilities that have befallen you.

The fourteenth commitment of mind training is to not point to others as the cause of a mistake that we ourselves have made.

15. Do not aim to win the race.

When you and others have mutually benefited some-one, do not say that you alone did so. And in the case where possessions are meant to be shared by you and others, abandon obtaining them by various means for yourself alone.

The fifteenth commitment of mind training is to not claim to have done something good alone when, in fact, we have done it together with others. In addition, when we receive something valuable that is meant to be shared with others, we should not keep it for ourselves by deceitfully trying to avoid sharing it.

16. Do not use perverse means.

Do not accept temporary defeat from others out of a desire for your own eventual good, and do not train your mind for the sake of pacifying an illness caused by spirits and such, since this would be doing so in order to achieve a trivial goal.

The sixteenth commitment of mind training is to not allow others to treat us badly now with the hope of receiving some kind of benefit later on. We also should not train in the mind of enlightenment for the purpose of avoiding harm from spirits nor preventing the retaliation of people we have harmed. To behave in such a way would be to act like someone who performs a profound ritual to achieve a trivial goal.

17. Do not turn a god into a demon.

To "turn a god into a demon" means to make a mistake in your way of relying on a god and, as a result of your devotion, to be killed by him. Analogously, if your pride, conceit, or hatred become stronger through meditating on mind training, this would be like turning a god into a demon. Do not allow this to happen.

The seventeenth commitment of mind training, that of *not turning a god into a demon,* generally refers to a situation in which, having previously relied on a particular mundane god to gain success, we make a mistake in our manner of devotion, and consequently that god, like a demon, begins to cause us harm and problems. Likewise, if the mental afflictions, anger, pride, jealousy, and so forth, actually increase instead of diminishing when we train in the mind of enlightenment, this is also said to be turning a god into a demon.

> *18. Do not seek [others'] suffering as a means to your
> own happiness.*

> Do not wish suffering upon others as a means to your
> own happiness, for example, by thinking that when
> your friends, relatives, Dharma companions, or others
> die, their food, wealth, texts, and so forth will come to
> you; that when a great meditator dies, his luck will
> come to you alone since you were peers; and that when
> an enemy dies, harm will no longer come to you.

The eighteenth commitment of mind training is to not be pleased with the happiness we gain at the expense of others' suffering. For example, when our friends and relatives die, we should not rejoice thinking that now we will receive their possessions. Nor when someone more famous than ourselves dies should we rejoice thinking that now we will gain his position or title. So too, when our enemies die, we should not rejoice, thinking how wonderful it is that there is now no one left to harm us.

· 7 ·

ADVICE REGARDING
MIND TRAINING

---

1. Perform all yogas with the one.

Everything you do—including eating, dressing, and the activities of walking, standing, lying, and sitting—should be sustained by the sole intention to benefit others.

All yogas, or activities, should be done with one mind, the mind of enlightenment. In other words, we should never be separated from the mind of enlightenment during any activity whatsoever.

2. Apply the one to all perverse oppressors.

Whenever the heartfelt desire to train your mind does not arise, for example, when you are harmed by spirits or when your afflictions are strong, turn away from the oppression of such a perverse mind and delight even more in training your mind.

Whenever we experience problems, such as sickness, harm caused by spirits, and strong afflictions, instead of becoming discouraged, we should inspire ourselves and develop our courage by remembering that such situations are very useful for the development of the mind of enlightenment. Thinking in this way, all our difficulties will become conditions that help us to generate energy and enthusiasm to complete the practice of mind training.

*3. Do the two activities, one at the beginning and one
at the end.*

Two [activities], that of developing a good motivation
at the beginning and that of dedicating and making
prayers at the end, are equally important. Immediately upon waking in the morning make a resolution,
thinking, "Today, without being separated from the two
precious minds [of enlightenment], I will render these
freedoms and endowments meaningful." Likewise,
maintain this [resolution] throughout the day with
mindfulness and introspection. At night check your
mind as you go to sleep, and if you find that you did
not transgress the mind training practices that day, then
rejoice. In addition, think, "Tomorrow, without being
separated from the mind training practices, I will also
render these freedoms and endowments meaningful."

Practitioners of mind training should always remember to begin
the day with the development of a positive motivation and to end
the day with a dedication of any merit accumulated. For this reason, when we wake up in the morning, we should generate the
mind of enlightenment; we should think, "Today, I will take as
much advantage as I possibly can of this precious human rebirth
without being separated from the mind of enlightenment." Then,
throughout the day we should constantly use mindfulness and
introspection to check whether we are actually maintaining the
motivation of the mind of enlightenment. Then, at night before
going to sleep, we should examine the various activities that we
have done throughout the day to determine whether we actually trained in the mind of enlightenment. If we discover that we
did something that was not in accordance with the mind training practice, we should immediately confess and purify it with the
four opponent forces. On the other hand, if we discover that we
did not transgress the mind training practices but did virtuous
actions, we should rejoice. Finally, just before going to sleep, we
should make a strong determination to continue the mind training practices the next day.

4. Be patient whichever of the two occurs.

Whenever you are particularly wealthy or have an
abundance of possessions and so forth, think of them

as being like illusions and, without arrogance, use them to benefit others as much as possible. On the other hand, whenever your mind is very depressed, think, "Nothing but water passes below me," and train your mind without discouragement in the precious mind of enlightenment by taking upon yourself the depression of other sentient beings.

During our lifetimes, we can experience very different situations; at one point we might be rich and famous, and at another time we might find ourselves poor and lonely. When things are going well, rather than being arrogant or haughty, we should reflect that our wealth, possessions, fame, and so forth are like illusions and use them to benefit others. On the contrary, when things are going badly, we should patiently endure this situation without becoming depressed and make ourselves happy by thinking how fortunate we are to have this precious human rebirth.

5. Guard the two at the risk of your life.

Since the commitments of Dharma in general, and the commitments of mind training in particular, are the root, guard them even more dearly than you do your life.

The commitments of Dharma include the individual liberation vows, the bodhisattva vows, and the tantric vows. The commitments of mind training are the eighteen commitments of mind training that support our practice of cherishing others more than ourselves. We should keep these two types of commitments even at the cost of our lives.

6. Train in the three difficult ones.

Initially, since it is difficult to be mindful of the afflictions, identify them. In the middle, since it is difficult to counteract them, generate the force of strong antidotes and strive to counteract them. At the end, since it is difficult to cut the continuity of the afflictions, think about their disadvantages in many ways and thereby cut their continuity.

Initially, it is difficult to identify, or recognize, the afflictions. Later, it is difficult to avert them. And finally, it is very difficult to cut their continuity or, in other words, to eliminate them completely.

Prior to beginning the mind training practices, our tendency when anything went wrong was to point our finger at external factors as the source of our problems. For this reason, it is initially difficult to recognize that we ourselves—our self-cherishing mind and our afflictions—are responsible for all our problems and errors. But, even after gaining the ability to recognize our afflictions, it remains very difficult to avert them. This is because we are unable to apply strong and effective antidotes to them once they have arisen in our minds. Subsequently, although we may have gained the ability to avert the afflictions, it remains difficult to totally eradicate them from our minds. Therefore, at this point it is very important to analyze the disadvantages of the afflictions by using many different lines of reasoning and by relying on relevant scriptural passages. For example, we can reflect that due to the mental afflictions, we have been forced to take rebirth again and again in cyclic existence; hence, if we do not eliminate them now, we will have to take rebirth endlessly into the future. Thinking like this, we should make a very strong determination to eliminate the afflictions once and for all.

7. Obtain the three principal causes.

a. The external condition: meeting an excellent guru who teaches the Great Vehicle path unmistakenly.

b. The internal condition: a qualified mind that, having acquired a body with the freedoms and endowments, has faith and is replete with wisdom, effort, and so forth.

c. The gathering together of conditions amenable to the accomplishment of Dharma without falling into either extreme with respect to food and clothes.

If these three [principal causes] are complete, rejoice; if they are not complete, put effort into creating the causes for completing them and pray from the depths of your heart that they quickly become complete.

There are three principal causes, or conditions, that enable us to engage in the mind training practices. The first cause is to meet a qualified guru able to perfectly and unmistakenly teach the path to enlightenment. The second cause is to have the right internal conditions: the freedoms and endowments of a perfect human rebirth together with intelligence and wisdom. The third cause is to live moderately without falling into either the extreme of leading an excessively luxurious life and being distracted by too many possessions or that of leading an excessively destitute life and experiencing the difficulties associated with a lack of even basic necessities.

We need to check whether we presently have these three causes for successful spiritual practice. If we discover that we do have them, we should be very happy and take advantage of this fortunate situation. If we find that we do not have them, we should work at creating the causes to acquire them.

8. *Cultivate the three without deterioration.*

One should do all [three] of the following:
a. Do not allow your appreciation of and respect for your guru to deteriorate, since he is the principal cause for the generation of qualities.

b. Do not allow your enthusiasm for training your mind to deteriorate.

c. Do not allow your mind to be separated from the two kinds of precious mind of enlightenment.

We should never allow our faith and respect for our guru to deteriorate because he or she is the source of all good qualities. Second, we should never allow our enthusiasm, joy, and courage concerning the practices of mind training to deteriorate. And third, we should never allow ourselves to be separated from the two kinds of mind of enlightenment, the conventional and the ultimate.

9. *[Possess the three without separation.]*

[Never part your body, speech, and mind from virtuous actions. Do not part your body from doing prostrations, making offerings, offering mandalas, circumambulating, and so forth; your speech from reciting requests, mantras, and verses of mind training; and your mind from meditating on the two minds of enlightenment, the cause for accumulating the two collections necessary for the attainment of the two bodies of a buddha.][12]

10. Train in purity and impartiality with respect to objects.

Train yourself in pure appearance with respect to both
sentient beings and inanimate objects. Then, without
partiality, train your mind.

We should train ourselves in impartiality toward all objects, the
animate and inanimate, by training ourselves in the appearance
of purity. To do this, we need to stop identifying some objects
as attractive and others as repulsive; we can do so by seeing the
environment as a pure land and all sentient beings as gods and
goddesses.

*11. Cherish all of the encompassing and profound
trainings.*

Train your mind without partiality toward all the sentient beings who take rebirth in the four modes.
Encompass whatever arises in your mind with your
mind training so that it does not remain mere words.

The four modes of rebirth are the various ways in which sentient
beings are born: (1) from a womb, (2) from an egg, (3) from heat
and moisture, and (4) miraculously. We should train ourselves
impartially to cherish all the sentient beings who are born in
these various ways.

12. Meditate constantly on the special cases.

Train with respect to five [special cases]:
  a. The [Three] Jewels, your gurus, and your parents
  are very kind, and are also delicate objects; hence, do
  not get angry with them.

  b. Although there are many causes to get angry with
  the family members with whom you constantly asso-
  ciate, do not react to them by showing anger.

  c. Abandon getting angry with the people who compete with you, whether they are lay men or lay
  women, monks or nuns.

  d. Even when you have not done anything to them,
  harmful beings may turn against you; if they do so,
  do not get angry with them.

e. If, in spite of never before having had a relationship of either acquaintance or intimacy with someone, you find yourself becoming repulsed, angry, and so forth merely upon hearing his or her name or seeing him or her, cultivate an especially affectionate love for that being.

In terms of special cases, the first point is to not get angry with the Three Jewels, our gurus, and our parents who are superior to us. The second point is to not get angry with the people with whom we live, such as our partner, parents, or friends. The third point is to not get angry with anyone, whether lay or ordained, who competes with us. The fourth point is to not get angry with beings who harm us, even though we have not done anything to harm them. And the fifth point is to meditate on love for those people who make us unhappy and uncomfortable when we just hear their names or see them from a distance.

13. Do not look for other conditions.

When favorable conditions come together, such as sufficient food and clothes, an absence of harm from humans and non-humans, good health, and so forth, train your mind. But if favorable conditions do not come together, do not stop training your mind—still train your mind.

Our practice of mind training should not depend on external conditions such that when we have plenty of food and clothing and so forth we practice mind training, but when we lack them we do not. In short, whether or not conditions are favorable, we should always practice mind training.

14. Practice the most important right now.

In the past, from beginningless lives up to the present, all the bodies we have taken have been without meaning. Now, having understood that of explaining and accomplishing, accomplishing is the most important, you should only practice mind training.

In the past we have taken many different kinds of rebirth, but because we wasted them, these lives have all been meaningless. Now that we have obtained a precious human rebirth with so much valuable potential, we should immediately try to put our study of mind training into practice so as to actually accomplish a transformation in our minds.

15. Avoid the distorted understandings.

Abandon [the six distorted understandings]:

a. A distorted understanding of patience is to lack patience in bearing hardships for Dharma, while patiently bearing hardships in order to overcome our enemies and protect our friends.

b. A distorted understanding of aspiration is to not aspire to accomplish the Dharma, while aspiring for the happiness and comfort of this life.

c. A distorted understanding of taste is to not taste the Dharma, such as the three, hearing, thinking, and meditating, while tasting the mundane happiness generated by attachment, hatred, and ignorance.

d. A distorted understanding of compassion is to not cultivate compassion for sentient beings who are tormented by suffering, while cultivating compassion for Dharma practitioners who are seen to lack a trifling bit of food and clothes.

e. A distorted understanding of a caring attitude is to not introduce people who are related to our friends and relatives to Dharma, while inducing them to take care of the belongings, which can be misused, of the [Three] Jewels and the Sangha and introducing them to methods for becoming wealthy in this life.

f. A distorted understanding of rejoicing is to not rejoice in the three times' roots of virtue of the buddhas, bodhisattvas, hearers, and solitary realizers, while rejoicing when our enemies suffer.

a. A distorted understanding of patience is to be unable to tolerate difficulties with respect to our Dharma practice but, on the other hand, to be able to bear all sorts of difficulties to accomplish worldly activities.

b. A distorted understanding of aspiration is to not aspire to practice Dharma while having a lot of energy to pursue temporal goals, such as those of obtaining food, clothing, and so forth.

c. A distorted understanding of taste is to prefer the taste of the mundane happiness generated by attachment, hatred, and ignorance over the taste of such Dharma activities as hearing, thinking, and meditating.

d. A distorted understanding of compassion is to not feel compassion for the sentient beings suffering in the three lower realms, but to become unhappy when seeing Dharma practitioners who do not have quite enough food, clothes, and so forth.

e. A distorted understanding of a caring attitude is to influence other people to misuse the belongings of a spiritual community and to lead them to create negative actions instead of inducing them to practice Dharma and encouraging them in such positive actions as hearing, thinking, and meditating.

f. A distorted understanding of rejoicing is to feel happy when others encounter problems and suffering, instead of rejoicing in the virtues of the buddhas, bodhisattvas, solitary realizers, and hearers.

16. Do not be erratic.

You should not train your minds at times and not train it at others. Instead, you should train your mind one-pointedly and continually, since this is the great path of all the buddhas of the three times.

We should not practice mind training for some time with exaggerated effort and then later, on becoming tired or discouraged, stop practicing it altogether for awhile. Instead, it is important that we train our minds steadily and continuously with a consistent amount of energy and effort.

17. Train continuously.

Resolve to train your mind continuously through completely transforming your mind into the mind training itself. Having made [this resolution], train your mind.

18. Attain liberation with the two, investigation and analysis.

Put effort into investigating which afflictions in your continuum are grosser and coarser. Then, having precisely analyzed the objects and causes and so forth that generate such afflictions, strive in the methods for not generating them.

We should constantly examine whether there are afflictions arising in our minds. On becoming aware that a certain affliction is present, we should try immediately to eradicate it by applying the appropriate antidote.

19. Do not boast.

Do not boast to others of your long-time practice of Dharma, your learnedness, nobility, and so forth, nor brag about the insignificant ways in which you have benefited others. Instead, act in accordance with what Drom Rinpoche taught, "Without expectations regarding human beings, make requests to the deities."

As a result of our mind training practice, we should never feel superior or special and consequently boast to others of our spiritual progress. Rather, we should find that, through our mind training practice, we are becoming more and more humble and increasingly able to see ourselves as inferior to others. Therefore, we should never boast of having done something beneficial for others, nor should we remind others of what we have done for them in the hope that they will feel obliged to help us in return. Instead, as Dromtönpa said, we should not have any expectations regarding human beings, but instead rely on and have confidence in the Three Jewels.

20. Refrain from retaliating.

If we exaggerate something of little importance into something great, such as others disparaging or insulting us, little improprieties in their way of speaking to us, their way of looking at us—whether it is perfect or faulty —or their way of acting, we will not [be able] to bear suffering and illness. Through meaninglessly ruminating upon [what happened] day and night until it no longer fits in our minds, we will retaliate. Since this will bring about our ruin, abandon ever generating such a mind.

When others insult or disparage us, look at us with an unpleasant expression, or speak badly to us, we should never resentfully hold a grudge against them but always keep our minds relaxed.

21. Do not act impetuously.

Do not show such demeanor as liking or not liking
trifling things — such behavior would annoy your
companions.

We should be careful not to be forever and suddenly changing
emotions, such as becoming instantly pleased and happy when
some small pleasant thing happens and, on the other hand,
immediately becoming angry and unhappy when some trivial
unpleasantness occurs. Instead, when we practice mind training,
we need to eliminate such fickle and impetuous behavior and
keep our minds controlled in all situations.

22. Do not wish for gratitude.

Practice Dharma without hope for expressions of gratitude regarding your practice, the benefit you have done
others, and so forth. Also practice without hope for
fame for yourself and so forth.

We should not engage in the mind training practices for the purpose of achieving happiness in our future lives nor to achieve
temporal happiness in this present life, such as gratitude, fame,
offerings, and so forth. Instead, we should practice mind training
in a meaningful and positive way so that it becomes Dharma
practice and the cause of enlightenment.

COLOPHON

Geshe Chekawa's Colophon

Geshe Chekawa, who had gained confidence in the mind of enlightenment, said:

The cause being my strong admiration, I ignored suffering and a bad reputation and requested these instructions for subduing self-grasping. Now even when I die, I will have no regrets.

Kadam geshe Chekawa, who had gained realizations and stability in the mind training practices, composed the text known as *Seven Point Mind Training.*

Gomo Tulku's Colophon

These instructions, the quintessence of the nectar, are of great benefit to the minds of everyone, including myself and others. This is because by meditating on emptiness alone without depending on the instructions for training in the mind of enlightenment, one cannot become a buddha. Even the state known as *Great Vehicle* is necessarily achieved in dependence on [the mind of enlightenment]. For these reasons, it is praised hundreds of times in many sutras and treatises. For example, glorious Chandrakirti said, "Mercy itself [is said to be the seed of] the perfect harvest of the conquerors."

I, who am called Gomo Tulku, having borrowed some of the mind training texts, wrote this memorandum in 1962 in Dharamsala (India). With great rejoicing from the depths of my heart in these texts, I did so mainly for the purpose of continually reminding myself of [the mind training practices]. I [composed this text] while making prayers thinking how wonderful if it were to become the cause for each and every one of my former mother sentient beings, who pervade space, to practice such a path. Also as a result of this [text], may

the precious teachings of the Conqueror spread and
flourish while remaining forever, and may the holy
beings who uphold [the teachings] live long, their lotus
feet remaining steadfast for hundreds of eons. May [this
text] also become the cause for myself and all sentient
beings, my former mothers, who pervade space, to
quickly generate in our continua the precious mind of
enlightenment, the realizations of thusness, and the two
stages of the path. May we thereby easily accomplish
unsurpassable great enlightenment, the precious state of
unification.

These instructions on mind training, the essence of all the Buddha's
teachings, are extremely beneficial for the minds of all sentient
beings. This is because by realizing emptiness alone without
developing the mind of enlightenment, we cannot attain buddhahood. In addition, whether we are actually practitioners of the
Great Vehicle depends entirely on whether we have developed the
mind of enlightenment.

Because the mind of enlightenment is so important and precious, it is very often praised by scholars such as Chandrakirti, who
said in his text *Entering the Middle Way,* "Mercy itself is said to
be the seed of the perfect harvest of the conquerors; the water for
its growth; and the ripe fruit that is a source of lasting enjoyment.
Therefore, I praise compassion right at the beginning." In fact,
there are many praises of the mind of enlightenment in both the
commentaries on sutra and tantra. Because I have so much admiration for the mind of enlightenment, I studied the mind training
texts extensively and composed this written commentary to
remind myself of these practices. I also made prayers that this
commentary would benefit many other sentient beings and dedicated the virtues created through composing this text for the long
life of all the holy beings who preserve the Buddha's teachings, for
the flourishing of the Buddha's teachings, and for all sentient
beings that they may quickly develop the mind of enlightenment
and attain buddhahood. You too should similarly dedicate the
virtues you have created by studying the practices of mind training.

APPENDIX

TIBETAN TEXT: ROOT VERSES
OF SEVEN POINT MIND TRAINING

ཐེག་པ་ཆེན་པོའི་བློ་སྦྱོང་དོན་བདུན་མའི་རྩ་བ།

ཐུགས་རྗེ་ཆེན་པོ་ལ་ཕྱག་འཚལ་ལོ། །མན་ངག་བདུད་རྩིའི་སྙིང་པོ་འདི། །གསེར་གླིང་པ་ནས་
བརྒྱུད་པ་ཡིན། །རྟོ་རྗེ་ཉི་མ་ལྟ་བུ་གདིང་བཞིན། །གཞུང་དོན་ལ་སོགས་ཤེས་པར་བྱ། །སྙིགས་
མ་ལྔ་པོ་བདོ་བ་འདི། །བྱང་ཆུབ་ལམ་དུ་བསྒྱུར་བ་ཡིན། །དང་པོ་སྔོན་འགྲོ་དག་ལ་བསླབ།
།ཁི་ལེན་ཐམས་ཅད་གཅིག་ལ་བདའ། །ཀུན་ལ་བཀའ་དྲིན་ཆེ་བར་སྐོམ། །གཏོང་ལེན་གཉིས་
པོ་སྤེལ་མར་སྦྱང་། །ལེན་པའི་གོ་རིམ་རང་ནས་བརྩམས། །དེ་གཉིས་རླུང་ལ་བསྐྱོན་པར་བྱ།
།ཡུལ་གསུམ་དུག་གསུམ་དགེ་རྩ་གསུམ། །ཐེས་ཀྱི་མན་ངག་མདོར་བསྡུས་པ། །དི་ལ་དུན་པ་
བསྐྱལ་བའི་ཕྱིར། །སྤྱོད་ལམ་ཀུན་ཏུ་ཚིག་གིས་སྦྱང་། །བདེན་པ་ཐོབ་ནས་གསང་བ་བསྟན།
།ཚོས་རྣམས་རྨི་ལམ་ལྟ་བུར་བསམ། །མ་སྐྱེས་རིག་པའི་གཤིས་ལ་དཔྱད། །གཉེན་པོ་ཉིད་
ཀྱང་རང་སར་གྲོལ། །ལམ་གྱི་ངོ་བོ་ཀུན་གཞིའི་ངང་ལ་བཞག །བར་དོར་སྒྱུ་མའི་སྐྱེས་
བུར་བྱ། །སྦྱོར་བཅུད་ཐེག་པ་གསང་བའི་ཀེ། །ཀྱེན་ངན་བྱང་ཆུབ་ལམ་དུ་བསྒྱུར། །འཁྲུལ་ལ་
གང་ཐུག་བསྒོམ་དུ་སྤྲད། །སྦྱོར་བ་བཞི་ལྡན་ཐབས་ཀྱི་མཆོག

།མན་ངག་སྙིང་པོ་མདོར་བསྡུས་པ། །སྟོབས་ལྔ་དག་དང་སྦྱར་བར་བྱ། །ཐེག་ཆེན་འཕོ་བའི་
གདམས་ངག་ནི། །སྟོབས་ལྔ་ཉིད་ཡིན་སྤྱོད་ལམ་གཅེས། །ཚོས་ཀུན་དགོངས་པ་གཅིག་ཏུ་
འདུས། །དཔང་པོ་གཉིས་ཀྱི་གཙོ་བོ་བཟུང་། །ཡིད་བདེ་འབའ་ཞིག་རྒྱུན་དུ་བསྟེན། །བྱུང་བའི་
ཚད་ནི་ལོག་པ་མིན། །འབྱོངས་རྟགས་ཆེན་པོ་ལྔ་ཡིན་ཡིས།

།ཡིངས་ཀྱང་ཐུབ་ན་འབྱོངས་པ་ཡིན། །སྤྱི་དོན་གསུམ་ལ་རྟག་ཏུ་བསླབ། །འདུན་པ་བསྒྱུར་ལ་
རང་སོར་བཞག །མན་ལག་ཉམས་པ་བརྗོད་མི་བྱ། །གཞན་ཕྱོགས་གང་ཡང་མི་བསམ་མོ།

།ཉིན་མོངས་གང་ཆེ་སྟོན་ལ་སྦྱང་། །འབྲས་བུ་རེ་བ་ཐམས་ཅད་སྤང་། །དུག་ཅན་གྱི་ཟས་སྤང་། གཞུང་བཟང་པོ་མི་བརྙེས། གཔགས་ངན་མི་ཉོན། འཕྲང་མི་སྐྱག གཉན་ལ་མི་དབབ། མཚོ་ཁལ་སྐྱང་ལ་མི་འགྲོ། མགྱོགས་ཀྱི་རྟ་མི་གཏོང་། སྟོ་ལོག་མི་བྱ། ཀླུ་བདུད་དུ་མི་དབབ། སྐྱིད་ཀྱི་ཡན་ལག་ཏུ་སྡུག་མི་འཚལ། རྣལ་འབྱོར་ཐམས་ཅད་གཅིག་གིས་བྱ། །ལོག་གནོན་ཐམས་ཅད་གཅིག་གིས་བྱ། །ཕོག་མཐའ་གཉིས་ལ་བྱ་བ་གཉིས། །གཉིས་པོ་གང་བྱུང་བཟོད་པར་བྱ། །གཉིས་པོ་སྟོག་དང་བརྫོས་ལ་བསྡང་། །དཀའ་བ་གསུམ་ལ་བསླབ་པར་བྱ། །ཀྱུ་མི་གཙོ་བོ་རྣམ་གསུམ་སྤང་། །ཉམས་པ་མེད་པ་རྣམ་གསུམ་བསྟེན།

།འདུལ་མེད་གསུམ་དང་ལྡན་པར་བྱ། །ཡུལ་ལ་ཕྱོགས་མེད་དག་ཏུ་སྤྱད། །ཁབ་དང་གཅིང་འབྱོངས་ཀུན་ལ་གཅེས། །བཀོལ་བ་རྣམས་ལ་དུག་ཏུ་བསྔོ། ཉིན་གཞན་དག་ལ་སློས་མི་བྱ། །ད་རེས་གཙོ་བོ་ཉམས་སུ་ལྡང་། །གོ་ལོག་མི་བྱ། རེས་འཇོག་མི་བྱ། དོལ་ཆོད་དུ་སྤྱད། །རྟོག་དཔྱོད་གཉིས་ཀྱིས་ཐབ་པར་བྱ། ཡུས་མ་བསྔོ། ཀོ་ལོང་མ་སྟོམ། ཡུད་ཙམ་པ་མི་བྱ། ཨོར་ཆེ་མི་འདོད། རང་གི་ཁོས་པ་མ་མང་བའི་རྒྱས། །སྒྲུག་བསྒལ་གཏམ་འན་ཁྱད་བསད་ནས། །བདག་འཛིན་འདུལ་བའི་གདམས་ང་ལུས། །ད་ནི་མི་ཡང་མི་འགྱུད་དོ།

NOTES

1. This refers to the six texts known as the "six Kadam texts" (bKa' gdams gzhung drug): *Ornament for the Mahayana Sutras* (Mahāyāna-sūtralamkāra), *Bodhisattva Grounds* (Bodhisattvabhūmi), *Engaging in the Bodhisattva Deeds* (Bodhisattvacharyāvatāra), *Compendium of Trainings* (Shikṣhāsamuchchaya), *Life Stories* (Jātakanidāna), and *Compilations of Indicative Verse* (Udānavarga).

2. The Tibetan that has been translated here as "sentient beings, your former mothers" (*ma rgan sems can*) could be translated more literally as elderly, or old, mother sentient beings; however, I feel that such a literal translation does not render the sense of the expression which is that all sentient beings have been our mothers at some time in our past lives.

3. The Tibetan *gtong len*, here translated as "taking and giving," could be more literally translated as "giving-taking" but I prefer to translate it as "taking and giving" in accordance with the order in which it is usually practiced, that is, taking followed by giving.

4. These are beings who in a previous life made perverse prayers; for example, King Langdarma of Tibet who in a previous life made prayers to destroy the Dharma and was subsequently reborn as a king who destroyed many monasteries and temples, killed monks and nuns, forced the ordained to disrobe, etc.

5. "A hundred tormas" refers to offerings of small round tormas. *Tsa-sur* is a burnt offering of butter, toasted barley flour, and six excellent [substances] (nutmeg (*dza ti*), saffron (*gur kum*), cloves (*li shi*), carda-mom (*ka ko la*), pomegranate seeds (*sug smel*), and sap/lime (*cu gang*)).

6. The ten Dharma activities are said to be either the ten perfections: (1) generosity, (2) morality, (3) patience, (4) effort, (5) concentration, (6) wisdom, (7) method, (8) prayer, (9) power, and (10) exalted wisdom;

or (1) writing the letters of the scriptures, (2) making offerings, (3) giving gifts, (4) listening to Dharma, (5) upholding Dharma, (6) reading Dharma, (7) explaining Dharma, (8) reciting Dharma, (9) thinking about the meaning of Dharma, and (10) meditating on the meaning of Dharma.

7. The auxiliary branches of the mind of enlightenment refer to great compassion, love, and so forth.

8. The meditation on the sevenfold causes and effect is a meditation for developing the mind of enlightenment and is composed of six causes — (1) the recognition of all sentient beings as having been one's mother, (2) remembering their kindness, (3) developing the wish to repay their kindness, (4) generating love, (5) generating compassion, and (6) generating the special attitude that accepts the responsibility to place all sentient beings in happiness and free them from suffering — and one effect, the altruistic attitude of the mind of enlightenment itself. See *Liberation in the Palm of Your Hand* for more details.

9. The term translated here as "hazardous" (*gnyan*) actually refers to spirits who reside in or near rocks, trees, water, and other such areas; these spirits are thought to cause diseases when disturbed.

10. Tormas are ritual cakelike offerings traditionally made of a doughy mixture of roasted barley flour (*tsampa*) and butter that is molded into various conical shapes and offered to deities, protectors, and mundane beings.

11. A *dzo* is a cross between a *dri* and a bull, or a cow and a *yak*.

12. This line and its commentary are missing in Gomo Rinpoche's text and were translated and added here from the Italian translation the source of which is unknown.

13. Footprints that appear in the ashes of realized beings are said to indicate the direction in which the incarnation is to be found. In fact, Gomo Tulku's incarnation was born three years later in Canada.

BIBLIOGRAPHY

SUTRAS

Life Stories
Jātakanidāna
sKyes pa rabs kyi gleng gzhi
P748, vol. 21.

SANSKRIT AND TIBETAN WORKS

Asanga (Thogs med) (4th century C.E.)
Bodhisattva Grounds
Yogacharyābhūmau bodhisattvabhūmi
rNal 'byor spyod pa'i sa las byang chub sems dpa'i sa
P5538, vol. 110, T4037.

Gomo Tulku (sgo mo sprul sku) (1922–1985)
Annotations to the Root Verses of Mind Training
bLo sbyong rtsa tshig la mchan 'grel
Unpublished.

Keutsang Jamyang Monlam (Ke'u tshang jam dbyangs smon lam)
Root Verses of Mind Training
bLo sbyong rtsa tshig
Included in the *Collected Works of Keutsang Jamyang Monlam*
   (Ke'u tshang sprul sku blo bzang jam dbyangs smon lam gyi
   gsung 'bum). Dharamsala: Library of Tibetan Works and
   Archives, 1984.

Langri Tangpa Dorje Sengge
(gLang ri thang pa rdo rje seng ges) (1054–1123)
Eight Verses on Mind Training
bLo sbyong tsig rkang brgyad ma lo rgyus dang bcad pa
Included in Sems dpa' chen po dkon mchog rgyal mtshan gyis
   phyogs bsgrigs mdzad pa'i blo sbyong brgya rtsa dang dkar chag
   gdung sel zla ba bcas. Compiled by dKon mchog rgyal mtsan.
   Dharamsala: Shes rig par khang, 1973. Translation by Brian
   Beresford, *Thought Transformation in Eight Stanzas.*
In Geshe Rabten and Geshe Dhargyey, *Advice from a Spiritual*

83

Friend, London: Wisdom, 1984.
Second translation by John Dunne. In Geshe Tsultim Gyeltsen,
Compassion: The Key to Great Awakening, Boston: Wisdom,
1997.

Maitreya (Byams-pa)
Ornament for Clear Realization
Abhisamayālamkāra
mNgon par rtogs pa'i rgyan
P5184, vol. 88.
Translated by E. Conze, *Abhisamayālankāra,* Serie Orientale
Roma VI (Rome: IS.M.E.O., July 1954).
Second translation by Thubten Jampa and George Churinoff,
Pomaia: Istituto Lama Tzong Khapa, unpublished.

Ornament for the Māhyāna Sutras
Mahāyānasūtralamkārakārikā
Theg pa chen po'i mdo sde'i rgyan gyi tshig le'ur byas pa
P5521, vol. 108.

Shantideva (Zhi-ba-lha)
Compendium of Trainings
Shikṣhāsamuchchayakārika
bsLab pa kun las btus pa'i tshig le'ur byas pa
P5336, vol. 102.
Translated by C. Bendall and W. H. D. Rouse, *Śikṣā Samuccaya,*
Delhi: Motilal, 1971.

Engaging in the Bodhisattva Deeds
Bodhisattvacharyāvatāra
Byang chub sems dpa'i spyod pa la 'jug pa
P5272, vol. 99.
English translations from the Sanskrit: Kate Crosby and Andrew
Skilton, *The Bodhicaryāvatāra,* Oxford: Oxford University
Press, 1995; Parmananda Sharma, *Śāntideva's Bodhi-
charyāvatāra,* New Delhi: Aditya Prakashan, 1990; Alan and
Vesna Wallace, *Guide to the Bodhisattva Way of Life,* Ithaca:
Snow Lion, 1997.
English translations from the Tibetan: Stephen Batchelor, *A
Guide to the Bodhisattva's Way of Life,* Dharamsala: Library of
Tibetan Works and Archives, 1979; Padmakara Translation
Group, *The Way of the Bodhisattva,* Boston: Shambhala, 1997.

Other Works

Batchelor, Stephen. *A Guide to the Bodhisattva's Way of Life*. Dharamsala: Library of Tibetan Works and Archives, 1979.

Bendall, C., and W. H. D. Rouse, *Śikṣā Samuccaya*. Delhi: Motilal, 1971.

Chattopadhyaya, Alaka. *Atisha and Tibet*. Delhi: Motilal, 1981.

Dhargyey, Ngawang. *An Anthology of Well-Spoken Advice*. Edited by Brian Beresford. Dharamsala: Library of Tibetan Works and Archives, 1982.

Dutt, Nalinaksha, ed. Bodhisattvabhumi (the fifteenth section of Asanga's *Yogacharyabhumi*). Tibetan Sanskrit Works Series, vol. 7. Patna: K. P. Jayaswal Research Institute, 1966.

Gyatso, Tenzin, The Fourteenth Dalai Lama. *The World of Tibetan Buddhism: An Overview of Its Philosophy and Practice*. Translated, edited, and annotated by Geshe Thupten Jinpa. Boston: Wisdom, 1995.

Gyeltsen, Geshe Tsultim. *Compassion: The Key to Great Awakening. Thought Training and the Bodhisattva Practices*. Boston: Wisdom, 1997.

Hopkins, Jeffrey. *Meditation on Emptiness*. Boston: Wisdom, 1996.

Kalsang, Lama Thubten. *Atisha*. Bangkok: Mahayana, 1983.

McDonald, Kathleen. *How to Meditate: A Practical Guide*. Boston: Wisdom, 1984.

Namkha Pel. *Mind Training Like the Rays of the Sun*. Translated by Brian Beresford. Dharamsala: Library of Tibetan Works and Archives, 1992.

Pabongka Rinpoche (Pha-bong-kha). *Liberation in Our Hand*, Parts One and Two. Translated by Geshe Lobsang Tharchin with Artemus B. Engle. Howell: Mahayana Sutra and Tantra Press, 1990, 1994.

Pabongka Rinpoche. *Liberation in the Palm of Your Hand*. Translated by Michael Richards. Boston: Wisdom, 1991.

Padmakara Translation Group. *The Way of the Bodhisattva*. Boston: Shambhala, 1997.

Rabten, Geshe. *The Essential Nectar*. London: Wisdom, 1984.

Rabten, Geshe, and Geshe Dhargyey. *Advice from a Spiritual Friend*. Translated by Brian Beresford. London: Wisdom, 1984.

Sparham, Gareth. *The Tibetan Dhammapada*. London: Wisdom, 1983.

Thurman, Robert A. F. *The Life and Teachings of Tsong Khapa*. Dharamsala: Library of Tibetan Works and Archives, 1982.

Wallace, Alan and Vesna. *Guide to the Bodhisattva Way of Life*. Ithaca: Snow Lion, 1997.

Wangchen, Geshe Namgyal. *Awakening the Mind: Basic Buddhist Meditations*. Boston: Wisdom, 1995.

Zopa Rinpoche, Lama Thubten. *Transforming Problems into Happiness*. Boston: Wisdom, 1993.

ABOUT THE AUTHOR

Gomo tulku (1922–1985) was the twenty-second incarnation of Sonam Rinchen, a highly realized Tibetan yogi who was one of the main disciples of the Indian mahasiddha Padampa Sanggye, a contemporary of the well-known Tibetan saint, Milarepa (1052–1135).

Gomo is the name of a mountainous locality in the Penpo region of central Tibet associated with the deity Chakrasamvara. Here Padampa Sanggye once lived and taught, and here his direct disciple Sonam Rinchen founded Gomo Hermitage with more than a hundred monks and a hundred meditators, and a nunnery of about seventy nuns. Among his disciples were many who attained enlightenment in that very lifetime. On his passing away, Sonam Rinchen's body was not cremated but placed inside a stupa within the monastery grounds where it remained without decomposing until its destruction by the Chinese.

Many of Sonam Rinchen's subsequent incarnations manifested as highly realized beings and qualified practitioners of Vajrayogini. When the twenty-first incarnation, who was recognized when he was already quite old, passed away, the administrators of Penpo Ganden Chökor Monastery requested Kyabje Pabongka Dechen Nyingpo to help them find his incarnation. This master identified the twenty-second incarnation of Sonam Rinchen to be a young child born in Penpo in the third month of the water-dog year (1922) to a family named Penpo Changrasar. This family, who belonged to the nobility, worked for the government and were also quite wealthy farmers. Following his official recognition as the incarnation of Sonam Rinchen, the young boy was escorted by a great procession to his monastery, Penpo Ganden Chökor, where he was received with great ceremony. A short time later, the Thirteenth Dalai Lama also confirmed that the five-year-old child was indeed the incarnation of Sonam Rinchen.

At his monastery in Penpo, the young incarnate lama, known as Gomo Tulku, studied the alphabet, reading, and writing, and memorized many of the monastery's prayers and rituals. From the ages of nine to eleven, he studied at the mountain hermitage of Pabongka Dechen Nyingpo, Trashi Chöling, where he received many initiations, transmissions, and oral instructions from Pabongka Rinpoche himself. Gomo Tulku then entered Sera Je Monastery where he studied the great treatises with Geshe Ngawang Jinpa.

During his years at Sera and his regular visits to his own monastery, Gomo Tulku memorized many tantric texts, received numerous initiations, and did many retreats. At the age of twenty, he received full ordination from Yongdzin Purchog Rinpoche (Purbuchog) and, at the age of twenty-five, completed the degree of Geshe Lingsel. He subsequently entered the Lower Tantric College where he studied and memorized the rituals of the deities associated with the four classes of tantra.

At the age of twenty-six, Gomo Tulku left the monastic life and married; however, he remained at Ganden Chökor Monastery in his position as head lama and continued to teach and confer initiations. At the beginning of the Chinese invasion of Tibet, Gomo Tulku, age thirty-six, departed for India with his wife and one-year-old daughter, Pema Yangkey. From 1960 to 1962, he served as the principal of the Tibetan school in Madras, during which time his second daughter, Yanki Chöden, was born. Gomo Tulku together with his family then moved north to Mussorie where for the next twenty-two years he served as the foster father of a children's home. For eighteen years, from 1964 onward, on the full moon of the fourth Tibetan month of Saka Dawa, Rinpoche organized and led an annual fasting retreat (*nyung-ne*) in which more than a hundred people regularly participated. He also introduced a yearly recitation of 100 million *om mani padme hum* mantras and oversaw the construction of a large prayer wheel containing more than 1.4 billion *mani* mantras housed in a building with walls lined with statues of the thousand buddhas of this fortunate eon.

Gomo Tulku received initiations principally from Kyabje Pabongka Rinpoche and Taggyab Rinpoche. In addition, he received initiations, teachings, and the transmissions of texts from His Holiness the Fourteenth Dalai Lama, Ling Rinpoche, and

Trijang Rinpoche, as well as from many other highly qualified teachers. Being the holder of many rare lineages of initiations, transmissions, and teachings, several of Rinpoche's gurus advised him to take particular care to preserve these lineages by passing them on to others. Aware of this, Lama Thubten Yeshe, spiritual founder of the Foundation for the Preservation of the Mahayana Tradition (FPMT), requested Gomo Tulku to pass on the rare lineages of initiations and transmissions to his Western disciples. Later, when he was very sick in Delhi, Lama Yeshe asked Lama Thubten Zopa Rinpoche to repeat this request. As a result, Gomo Tulku arrived at Istituto Lama Tzong Khapa, Pomaia, Italy at the beginning of January 1985. He subsequently taught at three Italian FPMT centers for a total of three and a half months, conferring entire collections of initiations, the transmission of the *Eight Thousand Stanza Perfection of Wisdom Sutra,* and tantric commentaries. In addition, he gave teachings on the stages of the path (*lam rim*) and mind training (*lo jong*) and taught ritual dancing, chanting, and torma making. During this time, many students, impressed by his tireless energy for teaching and his ability to inspire others to practice Dharma, became very devoted to him.

Gomo Tulku then spent a month and a half teaching and conferring initiations in FPMT centers in France, Spain, and Germany. At the end of May 1985, having concluded his European tour, Rinpoche unexpectedly decided to return to his family in India, canceling his scheduled teaching tour in Australia. Soon after his return to India, he was diagnosed with advanced liver cancer and on the fifteenth day of the sixth month of the Tibetan calendar (July 31, 1985) Gomo Tulku passed away. Disciples present at his death testified that rainbows appeared in the sky and that his body did not begin to decay, nor did it even change color, for three days, but remained sitting upright in the meditation posture. Following his cremation, people saw an image of Buddha in the ashes and the footprint of a small child pointing north.[13]

Signs during his lifetime also attested to Gomo Tulku's spiritual achievements; for example, on several occasions when Rinpoche was conferring initiations, rainbows and other auspicious signs were seen by those present. When the Fourteenth Dalai Lama first traveled to central Tibet from Amdo as a young child, he visited Gomo Tulku at his monastery. This was during the time of the autumn rains, and Rinpoche, having been asked to stop the heavy rain, did so for an entire week. Later on at the age of twenty-seven, while he was giving the transmission of the Kangyur to a large number of people, there was the threat of very heavy snowfall. Gomo Tulku was requested to prevent a possible calamity and complied by blessing hundreds of sacks of rock-salt that were then burned continually for several days over evergreen branches in a circular trench. The heavy snow did not fall. Also during Rinpoche's stay at Istituto Lama Tzong Khapa in the winter of 1985 unusual heavy snow fell and temperatures dropped below freezing, resulting in a loss of electricity and frozen water pipes. Rinpoche, having been requested to stop the snow, blessed some rock-salt that was then burned in the courtyard; soon after, a distinct circle of clear sky appeared above the Institute.

The twenty-third incarnation of Sonam Rinchen, Tenzin Dhonyag, was born August 8, 1988 in Montreal, Canada, to Yanki Chöden, the youngest daughter of Gomo Tulku. Officially recognized by His Holiness the Fourteenth Dalai Lama, he was enthroned at the age of seven by Lama Zopa Rinpoche at Istituto Lama Tzong Khapa, Pomaia, Italy, on September 7, 1995, and once again at Sera Monastery in South India on July 14, 1996. Like other young reincarnate lamas, Gomo Tulku, who received the ordination name of Tenzin Lhundrub Sangpo from His Holiness, will follow a traditional monastic education that will prepare him to continue inspiring and teaching others through his realization and knowledge of the Buddha's teachings.

INDEX

Note: Page numbers in bold refer to definitions of terms in the text.

THE FOUNDATION
FOR THE PRESERVATION
OF THE MAHAYANA TRADITION

THE FOUNDATION for the Preservation of the Mahayana Tradition (FPMT) is an international network of Buddhist centers and activities dedicated to the transmission of Mahayana Buddhism as a practiced and living tradition. The FPMT was founded in 1975 by Lama Thubten Yeshe and Lama Thubten Zopa Rinpoche. It is composed of Dharma teaching centers, monasteries, retreat centers, publishing houses, hospices, healing centers, and statue and stupa construction projects.

To receive a complete listing of these centers projects as well as news about the activities throughout this global network, please request a complimentary copy of MANDALA newsmagazine from:

FPMT International Office
PO Box 800
Soquel, California 95073 USA
Telephone: (408) 476-8435
Fax: (408) 476-4823
Email: fpmt@compuserve.com
www.fpmt.org

ABOUT WISDOM PUBLICATIONS

WISDOM PUBLICATIONS, a not-for-profit publisher, is dedicated to making available authentic Buddhist works for the benefit of all. We publish translations of the sutras and tantras, commentaries and teachings of past and contemporary Buddhist masters, and original works by the world's leading Buddhist scholars. We publish our titles with the appreciation of Buddhism as a living philosophy and with the special commitment to preserve and transmit important works from all the major Buddhist traditions.

If you would like more information or a copy of our mail-order catalog, please contact us at:

WISDOM PUBLICATIONS
199 Elm Street
Somerville, Massachusetts 02144 USA
Telephone: (617) 776-7416
Fax: (617) 776-7841
Email: info@wisdompubs.org
www.wisdompubs.org

THE WISDOM TRUST

AS A NOT-FOR-PROFIT PUBLISHER, Wisdom Publications is dedicated to the publication of fine Dharma books for the benefit of all sentient beings and dependent upon the kindness and generosity of sponsors in order to do so. If you would like to make a donation to Wisdom, please do so through our Somerville office. If you would like to sponsor the publication of a book, please write or e-mail us for more information.
Thank you.

Wisdom Publications is a non-profit, charitable 501(c)(3) organization and a part of the Foundation for the Preservation of the Mahayana Tradition (FPMT).